M000274252

The Law School Admission Council (LSAC) is a nonprofit corporation that provides unique, state-of-the-art admission products and services to ease the admission process for law schools and their applicants worldwide. More than 200 law schools in the United States, Canada, and Australia are members of the Council and benefit from LSAC's services.

LSAT, *The Official LSAT PrepTest*, *The Official LSAT SuperPrep*, *ItemWise*, and LSAC are registered marks of the Law School Admission Council, Inc. Law School Forums and LSAC Credential Assembly Service are service marks of the Law School Admission Council, Inc. *10 Actual, Official LSAT PrepTests*; *10 More Actual, Official LSAT PrepTests*; *The Next 10 Actual, Official LSAT PrepTests*; *The New Whole Law School Package*; *ABA-LSAC Official Guide to ABA-Approved Law Schools*; *Whole Test Prep Packages*; LLM Credential Assembly Service; ACES2; ADMIT-LLM; Law School Admission Test; and Law School Admission Council are trademarks of the Law School Admission Council, Inc.

LSAC fees, policies, and procedures relating to, but not limited to, test registration, test administration, test score reporting, misconduct and irregularities, Credential Assembly Service (CAS), and other matters may change without notice at any time. Up-to-date LSAC policies and procedures are available at LSAC.org, or you may contact our candidate service representatives.

ISBN-13: 978-0-942639-94-0
ISBN-10: 0-942639-94-4

Table of Contents

The Law School Admission Test is a half-day standardized test required for admission to all ABA-approved law schools, most Canadian law schools, and many non-ABA-approved law schools. It consists of five 35-minute sections of multiple-choice questions. Four of the five sections contribute to the test taker's score. These sections include one reading comprehension section, one analytical reasoning section, and two logical reasoning sections. The unscored section, commonly referred to as the variable section, typically is used to pretest new test questions or to preequate new test forms. The placement of this section in the LSAT will vary. A 35-minute writing sample is administered at the end of the test. The writing sample is not scored by LSAC, but copies are sent to all law schools to which you apply. The score scale for the LSAT is 120 to 180.

The LSAT is designed to measure skills considered essential for success in law school: the reading and comprehension of complex texts with accuracy and insight; the organization and management of information and the ability to draw reasonable inferences from it; the ability to think critically; and the analysis and evaluation of the reasoning and arguments of others.

The LSAT provides a standard measure of acquired reading and verbal reasoning skills that law schools can use as one of several factors in assessing applicants.

For up-to-date information about LSAC's services, go to LSAC.org.

Scoring

Your LSAT score is based on the number of questions you answer correctly (the raw score). There is no deduction for incorrect answers, and all questions count equally. In other words, there is no penalty for guessing.

■ Test Score Accuracy—Reliability and Standard Error of Measurement

Candidates perform at different levels on different occasions for reasons quite unrelated to the characteristics of a test itself. The accuracy of test scores is best described by the use of two related statistical terms: reliability and standard error of measurement.

Reliability is a measure of how consistently a test measures the skills being assessed. The higher the reliability coefficient for a test, the more certain we can be that test takers would get very similar scores if they took the test again.

LSAC reports an internal consistency measure of reliability for every test form. Reliability can vary from 0.00 to 1.00, and a test with no measurement error would have a reliability coefficient of 1.00 (never attained in practice). Reliability coefficients for past LSAT forms have ranged from .90 to .95, indicating a high degree of consistency for these tests. LSAC expects the reliability of the LSAT to continue to fall within the same range.

LSAC also reports the amount of measurement error associated with each test form, a concept known as the standard error of measurement (SEM). The SEM, which is usually about 2.6 points, indicates how close a test taker's observed score is likely to be to his or her true score. True scores are theoretical scores that would be obtained from perfectly reliable tests with no measurement error—scores never known in practice.

Score bands, or ranges of scores that contain a test taker's true score a certain percentage of the time, can be derived using the SEM. LSAT score bands are constructed by adding and subtracting the (rounded) SEM to and from an actual LSAT score (e.g., the LSAT score, plus or minus 3 points). Scores near 120 or 180 have asymmetrical bands. Score bands constructed in this manner will contain an individual's true score approximately 68 percent of the time.

Measurement error also must be taken into account when comparing LSAT scores of two test takers. It is likely that small differences in scores are due to measurement error rather than to meaningful differences in ability. The standard error of score differences provides some guidance as to the importance of differences between two scores. The standard error of score differences is approximately 1.4 times larger than the standard error of measurement for the individual scores.

Thus, a test score should be regarded as a useful but approximate measure of a test taker's abilities as measured by the test, not as an exact determination of his or her abilities. LSAC encourages law schools to examine the range of scores within the interval that probably contains the test taker's true score (e.g., the test taker's score band) rather than solely interpret the reported score alone.

■ Adjustments for Variation in Test Difficulty

All test forms of the LSAT reported on the same score scale are designed to measure the same abilities, but one test form may be slightly easier or more difficult than another. The scores from different test forms are made comparable through a statistical procedure known as equating. As a result of equating, a given scaled score earned on different test forms reflects the same level of ability.

■ Research on the LSAT

Summaries of LSAT validity studies and other LSAT research can be found in member law school libraries.

■ To Inquire About Test Questions

If you find what you believe to be an error or ambiguity in a test question that affects your response to the question, contact LSAC by e-mail: *LSATTS@LSAC.org*, or write to Law School Admission Council, Test Development Group, Box 40, Newtown, PA 18940-0040.

How This PrepTest Differs From an Actual LSAT

This PrepTest is made up of the scored sections and writing sample from the actual disclosed LSAT administered in June 2004. However, the reading comprehension section does not contain a comparative reading set (see page 5). Also, this PrepTest does not contain the extra, variable section that is used to pretest new test items of one of the three multiple-choice question types. The three multiple-choice question types may be in a different order in an actual LSAT than in this PrepTest. This is because the order of these question types is intentionally varied for each administration of the test.

The Question Types

The multiple-choice questions that make up most of the LSAT reflect a broad range of academic disciplines and are intended to give no advantage to candidates from a particular academic background.

The five sections of the test contain three different question types. The following material presents a general discussion of the nature of each question type and some strategies that can be used in answering them.

■ Analytical Reasoning Questions

Analytical reasoning items are designed to measure your ability to understand a structure of relationships and to draw logical conclusions about the structure. You are asked to make deductions from a set of statements, rules, or conditions that describe relationships among entities such as persons, places, things, or events. They simulate the kinds of detailed analyses of relationships that a law student must perform in solving legal problems. For example, a passage might describe four diplomats sitting around a table, following certain rules of protocol as to who can sit where. You must answer questions about the implications of the given information, for example, who is sitting between diplomats X and Y.

The passage used for each group of questions describes a common relationship such as the following:

- Assignment: Two parents, P and O, and their children, R and S, must go to the dentist on four consecutive days, designated 1, 2, 3, and 4;

- Ordering: X arrived before Y but after Z;

- Grouping: A manager is trying to form a project team from seven staff members—R, S, T, U, V, W, and X. Each staff member has a particular strength—writing, planning, or facilitating;

- Spatial: A certain country contains six cities and each city is connected to at least one other city by a system of roads, some of which are one-way.

Careful reading and analysis are necessary to determine the exact nature of the relationships involved. Some relationships are fixed (e.g., P and R always sit at the same table). Other relationships are variable (e.g., Q must be assigned to either table 1 or table 3). Some relationships that are not stated in the conditions are implied by and can be deduced from those that are stated. (e.g., If one condition about books on a shelf specifies that Book L is to the left of Book Y, and another specifies that Book P is to the left of Book L, then it can be deduced that Book P is to the left of Book Y.)

No formal training in logic is required to answer these questions correctly. Analytical reasoning questions are intended to be answered using knowledge, skills, and reasoning ability generally expected of college students and graduates.

Suggested Approach

Some people may prefer to answer first those questions about a passage that seem less difficult and then those that seem more difficult. In general, it is best not to start another passage before finishing one begun earlier, because much time can be lost in returning to a passage and reestablishing familiarity with its relationships. Do not assume that, because the conditions for a set of questions look long or complicated, the questions based on those conditions will necessarily be especially difficult.

Reading the passage. In reading the conditions, do not introduce unwarranted assumptions. For instance, in a set establishing relationships of height and weight among the members of a team, do not assume that a person who is taller than another person must weigh more than that person. All the information needed to answer each question is provided in the passage and the question itself.

The conditions are designed to be as clear as possible; do not interpret them as if they were intended to trick you. For example, if a question asks how many people could be eligible to serve on a committee, consider only those people named in the passage unless directed otherwise. When in doubt, read the conditions in their most obvious sense. Remember, however, that the language in the conditions is intended to be read for precise meaning. It is essential to pay particular attention to words that describe or limit relationships, such as "only," "exactly," "never," "always," "must be," "cannot be," and the like.

The result of this careful reading will be a clear picture of the structure of the relationships involved, including the kinds of relationships permitted, the participants in the relationships, and the range of actions or attributes allowed by the relationships for these participants.

Questions are independent. Each question should be considered separately from the other questions in its set; no information, except what is given in the original conditions, should be carried over from one question to another. In some cases a question will simply ask for conclusions to be drawn from the conditions as originally given. Some questions may, however, add information to the original conditions or temporarily suspend one of the original conditions for the purpose of that question only. For example, if Question 1 adds the information "if P is sitting at table 2 ...," this information should NOT be carried over to any other question in the group.

Highlighting the text; using diagrams. Many people find it useful to underline key points in the passage and in each question. In addition, it may prove very helpful to draw a diagram to assist you in finding the solution to the problem.

In preparing for the test, you may wish to experiment with different types of diagrams. For a scheduling problem, a calendar-like diagram may be helpful. For a spatial relationship problem, a simple map can be a useful device.

Even though some people find diagrams to be very helpful, other people seldom use them. And among those who do regularly use diagrams in solving these problems, there is by no means universal agreement on which kind of diagram is best for which problem or in which cases a diagram is most useful. Do not be concerned if a particular problem in the test seems to be best approached without the use of a diagram.

■ Logical Reasoning Questions

Logical reasoning questions evaluate your ability to understand, analyze, criticize, and complete a variety of arguments. The arguments are contained in short passages taken from a variety of sources, including letters to the editor, speeches, advertisements, newspaper articles and editorials, informal discussions and conversations, as well as articles in the humanities, the social sciences, and the natural sciences.

Each logical reasoning question requires you to read and comprehend a short passage, then answer one or two questions about it. The questions test a variety of abilities involved in reasoning logically and thinking critically. These include:

- recognizing the point or issue of an argument or dispute;

- detecting the assumptions involved in an argumentation or chain of reasoning;

- drawing reasonable conclusions from given evidence or premises;

- identifying and applying principles;

- identifying the method or structure of an argument or chain of reasoning;

- detecting reasoning errors and misinterpretations;

- determining how additional evidence or argumentation affects an argument or conclusion; and

- identifying explanations and recognizing resolutions of conflicting facts or arguments.

The questions do not presuppose knowledge of the terminology of formal logic. For example, you will not be expected to know the meaning of specialized terms such as "ad hominem" or "syllogism." On the other hand, you will be expected to understand and critique the reasoning contained in arguments. This requires that you possess, at a minimum, a college-level understanding of widely used concepts such as argument, premise, assumption, and conclusion.

Suggested Approach

Read each question carefully. Make sure that you understand the meaning of each part of the question. Make sure that you understand the meaning of each answer choice and the ways in which it may or may not relate to the question posed.

Do not pick a response simply because it is a true statement. Although true, it may not answer the question posed.

Answer each question on the basis of the information that is given, even if you do not agree with it. Work within the context provided by the passage. LSAT questions do not involve any tricks or hidden meanings.

■ Reading Comprehension Questions

The purpose of reading comprehension questions is to measure your ability to read, with understanding and insight, examples of lengthy and complex materials similar to those commonly encountered in law school work. The reading comprehension section of the LSAT contains four sets of reading questions, each consisting of a selection of reading material followed by five to eight questions. The reading selection in three of the four sets consists of a single reading passage of approximately 450 words in length. The other set contains two related shorter passages. Sets with two passages are a new variant of reading comprehension, called comparative reading, which was introduced into the reading comprehension section in June 2007. See "Comparative Reading" below for more information.

Reading selections for reading comprehension questions are drawn from subjects such as the humanities, the social sciences, the biological and physical sciences, and issues related to the law. Reading comprehension questions require you to read carefully and accurately, to determine the relationships among the various parts of the reading selection, and to draw reasonable inferences from the material in the selection. The questions may ask about the following characteristics of a passage or pair of passages:

- the main idea or primary purpose;

- the meaning or purpose of words or phrases used;

- information explicitly stated;

- information or ideas that can be inferred;

- the organization or structure;

- the application of information in a passage to a new context; and

- the author's attitude as it is revealed in the tone of a passage or the language used.

Suggested Approach

Since reading selections are drawn from many different disciplines and sources, you should not be discouraged if you encounter material with which you are not familiar. It is important to remember that questions are to be answered exclusively on the basis of the information provided in the selection. There is no particular knowledge that you are expected to bring to the test, and you should not make inferences based on any prior knowl-

edge of a subject that you may have. You may, however, wish to defer working on a set of questions that seems particularly difficult or unfamiliar until after you have dealt with sets you find easier.

Strategies. In preparing for the test, you should experiment with different strategies and decide which work most effectively for you. These include:

- reading the selection very closely and then answering the questions;

- reading the questions first, reading the selection closely, and then returning to the questions; or

- skimming the selection and questions very quickly, then rereading the selection closely and answering the questions.

Remember that your strategy must be effective for you under timed conditions.

Reading the selection. Whatever strategy you choose, you should give the passage or pair of passages at least one careful reading before answering the questions. Try to distinguish main ideas from supporting ideas, and opinions or attitudes from factual, objective information. Note transitions from one idea to the next and examine the relationships among the different ideas or parts of a passage, or between the two passages in comparative reading sets. Consider how and why an author makes points and draws conclusions. Be sensitive to implications of what the passages say.

You may find it helpful to mark key parts of passages. For example, you might underline main ideas or important arguments, and you might circle transitional words—"although," "nevertheless," "correspondingly," and the like—that will help you map the structure of a passage. Moreover, you might note descriptive words that will help you identify an author's attitude toward a particular idea or person.

Answering the Questions

- Always read all the answer choices before selecting the best answer. The best answer choice is the one that most accurately and completely answers the question being posed.

- Respond to the specific question being asked. Do not pick an answer choice simply because it is a true statement. For example, picking a true statement might yield an incorrect answer to a question in which you are asked to identify an author's position on an issue, since here you are not being asked to evaluate the truth of the author's position but only to correctly identify what that position is.

- Answer the questions only on the basis of the information provided in the selection. Your own views, interpretations, or opinions, and those you have heard from others, may sometimes conflict with those expressed in a reading selection; however, you are expected to work within the context provided by the reading selection. You should not expect to agree with everything you encounter in reading comprehension passages.

■ Comparative Reading

As of the June 2007 administration, LSAC introduced a new variant of reading comprehension, called comparative reading, as one of the four sets in the LSAT reading comprehension section. In general, comparative reading questions are similar to traditional reading comprehension questions, except that comparative reading questions are based on two shorter passages instead of one longer passage. The two passages together are of roughly the same length as one reading comprehension passage, so the total amount of reading in the reading comprehension section remains essentially the same. A few of the questions that follow a comparative reading passage pair might concern only one of the two passages, but most will be about both passages and how they relate to each other.

Comparative reading questions reflect the nature of some important tasks in law school work, such as understanding arguments from multiple texts by applying skills of comparison, contrast, generalization, and synthesis to the texts. The purpose of comparative reading is to assess this important set of skills directly.

What Comparative Reading Looks Like

The two passages in a comparative reading set—labeled "Passage A" and "Passage B"—discuss the same topic or related topics. The topics fall into the same academic categories traditionally used in reading comprehension: humanities, natural sciences, social sciences, and issues related to the law. Like traditional reading comprehension passages, comparative reading passages are complex and generally involve argument. The two passages in a comparative reading pair are typically adapted from two different published sources written by two different authors. They are usually independent of each other, with neither author responding directly to the other.

As you read the pair of passages, it is helpful to try to determine what the central idea or main point of each passage is, and to determine how the passages relate to each other. The passages will relate to each other in various ways. In some cases, the authors of the passages will be in general agreement with each other, while in others their views will be directly opposed. Passage pairs may also exhibit more complex types of relationships: for example, one passage might articulate a set of principles, while the other passage applies those or similar principles to a particular situation.

Questions that are concerned with only one of the passages are essentially identical to traditional reading comprehension questions. Questions that address both passages test the same fundamental reading skills as traditional reading comprehension questions, but the skills are applied to two texts instead of one. You may be asked to identify a main purpose shared by both passages, a statement with which both authors would agree, or a similarity or dissimilarity in the structure of the arguments in the two passages. The following are additional examples of comparative reading questions:

- Which one of the following is the central topic of each passage?

- Both passages explicitly mention which one of the following?

- Which one of the following statements is most strongly supported by both passages?

Which one of the following most accurately describes the attitude expressed by the author of passage B toward the overall argument in passage A?

- The relationship between passage A and passage B is most analogous to the relationship in which one of the following?

This is not a complete list of the sorts of questions you may be asked in a comparative reading set, but it illustrates the range of questions you may be asked.

For a sample comparative reading set, including explanations of the answers, go to LSAC.org, search for "comparative reading" in the search bar, and select "Preparing for the LSAT (PDF)."

The Writing Sample

Test takers are given 35 minutes to complete the brief writing exercise, which is not scored but is used by law school admission personnel to assess writing skill. Read the topic carefully. You will probably find it best to spend a few minutes considering the topic and organizing your thoughts before you begin writing. **Do not write on a topic other than the one specified. Writing on a topic of your own choice is not acceptable.**

There is no "right" or "wrong" position on the writing sample topic. Law schools are interested in how skillfully you support the position you take and how clearly you express that position. How well you write is much more important than how much you write. No special knowledge is required or expected. Law schools are interested in organization, vocabulary, and writing mechanics. They understand the short time available to you and the pressure under which you are writing.

Confine your writing to the blocked, lined area on the front and back of the Writing Sample Response Sheet. Only that area will be reproduced for laws schools. Be sure that your handwriting is legible.

Current information can be found at LSAC.org.

Taking the PrepTest Under Simulated LSAT Conditions

One important way to prepare for the LSAT is to simulate the day of the test by taking a practice test under actual time constraints. Taking a practice test under timed conditions helps you to estimate the amount of time you can afford to spend on each question in a section and to determine the question types on which you may need additional practice.

Since the LSAT is a timed test, it is important to use your allotted time wisely. During the test, you may work only on the section designated by the test supervisor. You cannot devote extra time to a difficult section and make up that time on a section you find easier. In pacing yourself, and checking your answers, you should think of each section of the test as a separate minitest.

Be sure that you answer every question on the test. When you do not know the correct answer to a question, first eliminate the responses that you know are incorrect, then make your best guess among the remaining choices. Do not be afraid to guess as there is no penalty for incorrect answers.

When you take a practice test, abide by all the requirements specified in the directions and keep strictly within the specified time limits. Work without a rest period. When you take an actual test you will have only a short break—usually 10-15 minutes—after SECTION III. When taken under conditions as much like actual testing conditions as possible, a sample test provides very useful preparation for taking the LSAT.

Official directions for the four multiple-choice sections and the writing sample are included in this PrepTest so that you can approximate actual testing conditions as you practice.

To take the test:

- Set a timer for 35 minutes. Answer all the questions in SECTION I of this PrepTest. Stop working on that section when the 35 minutes have elapsed.

- Repeat, allowing yourself 35 minutes each for sections II, III, and IV.

- Set the timer for 35 minutes, then prepare your response to the writing sample for this PrepTest.

- Refer to "Computing Your Score" for the PrepTest for instruction on evaluating your performance. An answer key is provided for that purpose.

The practice test that follows consists of four sections corresponding to the four scored sections of the June 2004 LSAT. Also reprinted is the June 2004 unscored writing sample topic.

General Directions for the LSAT Answer Sheet

The actual testing time for this portion of the test will be 2 hours 55 minutes. There are five sections, each with a time limit of 35 minutes. The supervisor will tell you when to begin and end each section. If you finish a section before time is called, you may check your work on that section <u>only</u>; do not turn to any other section of the test book and do not work on any other section either in the test book or on the answer sheet.

There are several different types of questions on the test, and each question type has its own directions. <u>Be sure you understand the directions for each question type before attempting to answer any questions in that section.</u>

Not everyone will finish all the questions in the time allowed. Do not hurry, but work steadily and as quickly as you can without sacrificing accuracy. You are advised to use your time effectively. If a question seems too difficult, go on to the next one and return to the difficult question after completing the section. MARK THE BEST ANSWER YOU CAN FOR EVERY QUESTION. NO DEDUCTIONS WILL BE MADE FOR WRONG ANSWERS. YOUR SCORE WILL BE BASED ONLY ON THE NUMBER OF QUESTIONS YOU ANSWER CORRECTLY.

ALL YOUR ANSWERS MUST BE MARKED ON THE ANSWER SHEET. Answer spaces for each question are lettered to correspond with the letters of the potential answers to each question in the test book. After you have decided which of the answers is correct, blacken the corresponding space on the answer sheet. BE SURE THAT EACH MARK IS BLACK AND COMPLETELY FILLS THE ANSWER SPACE. Give only one answer to each question. If you change an answer, be sure that all previous marks are <u>erased completely</u>. Since the answer sheet is machine scored, incomplete erasures may be interpreted as intended answers. ANSWERS RECORDED IN THE TEST BOOK WILL NOT BE SCORED.

There may be more questions noted on this answer sheet than there are questions in a section. Do not be concerned but be certain that the section and number of the question you are answering matches the answer sheet section and question number. Additional answer spaces in any answer sheet section should be left blank. Begin your next section in the number one answer space for that section.

LSAC takes various steps to ensure that answer sheets are returned from test centers in a timely manner for processing. In the unlikely event that an answer sheet(s) is not received, LSAC will permit the examinee to either retest at no additional fee or to receive a refund of his or her LSAT fee. THESE REMEDIES ARE THE EXCLUSIVE REMEDIES AVAILABLE IN THE UNLIKELY EVENT THAT AN ANSWER SHEET IS NOT RECEIVED BY LSAC.

Score Cancellation

Complete this section only if you are absolutely certain you want to cancel your score. A CANCELLATION REQUEST CANNOT BE RESCINDED. IF YOU ARE AT ALL UNCERTAIN, YOU SHOULD <u>NOT</u> COMPLETE THIS SECTION.

To cancel your score from this administration, you **must:**

A. fill in both ovals here ..... ◯ ◯
   AND

B. read the following statement. Then sign your name and enter the date. **YOUR SIGNATURE ALONE IS NOT SUFFICIENT FOR SCORE CANCELLATION. BOTH OVALS ABOVE MUST BE FILLED IN FOR SCANNING EQUIPMENT TO RECOGNIZE YOUR REQUEST FOR SCORE CANCELLATION.**

I certify that I wish to cancel my test score from this administration. I understand that my request is irreversible and that my score will not be sent to me or to the law schools to which I apply.

Sign your name in full
_____

Date
_____

HOW DID YOU PREPARE FOR THE LSAT?
(Select all that apply.)

Responses to this item are voluntary and will be used for statistical research purposes only.

◯ By studying the free sample questions available on LSAC's website.
◯ By taking the free sample LSAT available on LSAC's website.
◯ By working through official LSAT *PrepTests, ItemWise,* and/or other LSAC test prep products.
◯ By using LSAT prep books or software **not** published by LSAC.
◯ By attending a commercial test preparation or coaching course.
◯ By attending a test preparation or coaching course offered through an undergraduate institution.
◯ Self study.
◯ Other preparation.
◯ No preparation.

CERTIFYING STATEMENT
Please write the following statement. Sign and date.

I certify that I am the examinee whose name appears on this answer sheet and that I am here to take the LSAT for the sole purpose of being considered for admission to law school. I further certify that I will neither assist nor receive assistance from any other candidate, and I agree not to copy or retain examination questions or to transmit them to or discuss them with any other person in any form.

_____
_____
_____
_____
_____
_____
_____
_____

SIGNATURE: _____   TODAY'S DATE: ____ / ____ / ____
                                                        MONTH DAY YEAR

INSTRUCTIONS FOR COMPLETING THE BIOGRAPHICAL AREA ARE ON THE BACK COVER OF YOUR TEST BOOKLET.
USE ONLY A NO. 2 OR HB PENCIL TO COMPLETE THIS ANSWER SHEET. DO NOT USE INK.

A

USE A NO. 2 OR HB PENCIL ONLY

● **Right Mark**   ⊘ⓧ⊙ **Wrong Marks**

1 LAST NAME | FIRST NAME | MI

2 SOCIAL SECURITY/ SOCIAL INSURANCE NO.

3 LSAC ACCOUNT NUMBER

L

4 DATE OF BIRTH

MONTH	DAY	YEAR
Jan		
Feb		
Mar		
Apr		
May		
June		
July		
Aug		
Sept		
Oct		
Nov		
Dec		

5 RACIAL/ETHNIC DESCRIPTION
Mark one or more
- 1 Aboriginal/TSI Australian
- 2 Amer. Indian/Alaska Native
- 3 Asian
- 4 Black/African American
- 5 Canadian Aboriginal
- 6 Caucasian/White
- 7 Hispanic/Latino
- 8 Native Hawaiian/ Other Pacific Islander
- 9 Puerto Rican

6 GENDER
- Male
- Female

7 DOMINANT LANGUAGE
- English
- Other

8 ENGLISH FLUENCY
- Yes   - No

9 TEST BOOK SERIAL NO.

10 TEST FORM

11 TEST DATE
MONTH / DAY / YEAR

12 CENTER NUMBER

13 TEST FORM CODE

Law School Admission Test

Mark one and only one answer to each question. Be sure to fill in completely the space for your intended answer choice. If you erase, do so completely. Make no stray marks.

SECTION 1 (1–30, A B C D E)

SECTION 2 (1–30, A B C D E)

SECTION 3 (1–30, A B C D E)

SECTION 4 (1–30, A B C D E)

SECTION 5 (1–30, A B C D E)

14 PLEASE PRINT ALL INFORMATION

LAST NAME   FIRST

SOCIAL SECURITY/SOCIAL INSURANCE NO.

DATE OF BIRTH

MAILING ADDRESS

NOTE: If you have a new address, you must write LSAC at Box 2000-C, Newtown, PA 18940 or call 215.968.1001.

FOR LSAC USE ONLY		
LR	LW	LCS

● Ⓑ

SECTION I

Time—35 minutes

28 Questions

Directions: Each passage in this section is followed by a group of questions to be answered on the basis of what is <u>stated</u> or <u>implied</u> in the passage. For some of the questions, more than one of the choices could conceivably answer the question. However, you are to choose the <u>best</u> answer; that is, the response that most accurately and completely answers the question, and blacken the corresponding space on your answer sheet.

The accumulation of scientific knowledge regarding the environmental impact of oil well drilling in North America has tended to lag behind the actual drilling of oil wells. Most attempts to

(5) regulate the industry have relied on hindsight: the need for regulation becomes apparent only after undesirable events occur. The problems associated with oil wells' potential contamination of groundwater—fresh water within the earth that

(10) supplies wells and springs—provide a case in point.

When commercial drilling for oil began in North America in the mid-nineteenth century, regulations reflected the industry's concern for the purity of the wells' oil. In 1893, for example, regulations were

(15) enacted specifying well construction requirements to protect oil and gas reserves from contamination by fresh water. Thousands of wells were drilled in such a way as to protect the oil, but no thought was given to the possibility that the groundwater itself might need

(20) protection until many drinking-water wells near the oil well sites began to produce unpotable, oil-contaminated water.

The reason for this contamination was that groundwater is usually found in porous and

(25) permeable geologic formations near the earth's surface, whereas petroleum and unpotable saline water reservoirs are generally found in similar formations but at greater depths. Drilling a well creates a conduit connecting all the formations that it

(30) has penetrated. Consequently, without appropriate safeguards, wells that penetrate both groundwater and oil or saline water formations inevitably contaminate the groundwater. Initial attempts to prevent this contamination consisted of sealing off the

(35) groundwater formations with some form of protective barrier to prevent the oil flowing up the well from entering or mixing with the natural groundwater reservoir. This method, which is still in use today, initially involved using hollow trees to seal off the

(40) groundwater formations; now, however, large metal pipe casings, set in place with cement, are used.

Regulations currently govern the kinds of casing and cement that can be used in these practices; however, the hazards of insufficient knowledge

(45) persist. For example, the long-term stability of this

way of protecting groundwater is unknown. The protective barrier may fail due to corrosion of the casing by certain fluids flowing up the well, or because of dissolution of the cement by these fluids.

(50) The effects of groundwater bacteria, traffic vibrations, and changing groundwater chemistry are likewise unassessed. Further, there is no guarantee that wells drilled in compliance with existing regulations will not expose a need for research in additional areas: on

(55) the west coast of North America, a major disaster recently occurred because a well's location was based on a poor understanding of the area's subsurface geology. Because the well was drilled in a channel accessing the ocean, not only was the area's

(60) groundwater completely contaminated, but widespread coastal contamination also occurred, prompting international concern over oil exploration and initiating further attempts to refine regulations.

1. Which one of the following most accurately states the main point of the passage?

(A) Although now recognized as undesirable, occasional groundwater contamination by oil and unpotable saline water is considered to be inevitable wherever drilling for oil occurs.

(B) Widespread coastal contamination caused by oil well drilling in North America has prompted international concern over oil exploration.

(C) Hindsight has been the only reliable means available to regulation writers responsible for devising adequate safeguard regulations to prevent environmental contamination associated with oil well drilling.

(D) The risk of environmental contamination associated with oil well drilling continues to exist because safeguard regulations are often based on hindsight and less-than-sufficient scientific information.

(E) Groundwater contamination associated with oil well drilling is due in part to regulations designed to protect the oil from contamination by groundwater and not the groundwater from contamination by oil.

GO ON TO THE NEXT PAGE.

2. The passage states which one of the following about underground oil reservoirs?

   (A)   They are usually located in areas whose subsurface geology is poorly understood.

   (B)   They are generally less common in coastal regions.

   (C)   They are usually located in geologic formations similar to those in which gas is found.

   (D)   They are often contaminated by fresh or saline water.

   (E)   They are generally found at greater depths than groundwater formations.

3. The author's attitude regarding oil well drilling regulations can most accurately be described as

   (A)   cynical that future regulatory reform will occur without international concern

   (B)   satisfied that existing regulations are adequate to prevent unwarranted tradeoffs between resource collection and environmental protection

   (C)   concerned that regulatory reform will not progress until significant undesirable events occur

   (D)   optimistic that current scientific research will spur regulatory reform

   (E)   confident that regulations will eventually be based on accurate geologic understandings

4. The author uses the phrase "the hazards of insufficient knowledge" (line 44) primarily in order to refer to the risks resulting from

   (A)   a lack of understanding regarding the dangers to human health posed by groundwater contamination

   (B)   a failure to comprehend the possible consequences of drilling in complex geologic systems

   (C)   poorly tested methods for verifying the safety of newly developed technologies

   (D)   an inadequate appreciation for the difficulties of enacting and enforcing environmental regulations

   (E)   a rudimentary understanding of the materials used in manufacturing metal pipe casings

5. Based on the information in the passage, if a prospective oil well drilled near a large city encounters a large groundwater formation and a small saline water formation, but no oil, which one of the following statements is most likely to be true?

   (A)   Groundwater contamination is unlikely because the well did not strike oil and hence will not be put in operation.

   (B)   Danger to human health due to groundwater contamination is unlikely because large cities generally have more than one source of drinking water.

   (C)   Groundwater contamination is likely unless the well is plugged and abandoned.

   (D)   Groundwater contamination is unlikely because the groundwater formation's large size will safely dilute any saline water that enters it.

   (E)   The risk of groundwater contamination can be reduced if casing is set properly and monitored routinely for breakdown.

GO ON TO THE NEXT PAGE.

In many bilingual communities of Puerto Rican Americans living in the mainland United States, people use both English and Spanish in a single conversation, alternating between them smoothly and
(5) frequently even within the same sentence. This practice—called code-switching—is common in bilingual populations. While there are some cases that cannot currently be explained, in the vast majority of cases subtle factors, either situational or rhetorical,
(10) explain the use of code-switching.

Linguists say that most code-switching among Puerto Rican Americans is sensitive to the social contexts, which researchers refer to as domains, in which conversations take place. The main
(15) conversational factors influencing the occurrence of code-switching are setting, participants, and topic. When these go together naturally they are said to be congruent; a set of three such congruent factors constitutes a conversational situation. Linguists
(20) studying the choice between Spanish and English among a group of Puerto Rican American high school students classified their conversational situations into five domains: family, friendship, religion, education, and employment. To test the effects of these domains
(25) on code-switching, researchers developed a list of hypothetical situations made up of two of the three congruent factors, or of two incongruent factors, approximating an interaction in one of the five domains. The researchers asked the students to
(30) determine the third factor and to choose which mix of language—on a continuum from all English to all Spanish—they would use in that situation. When given two congruent factors, the students easily supplied the third congruent factor and strongly
(35) agreed among themselves about which mix they would use. For instance, for the factors of participants "parent and child" and the topic "how to be a good son or daughter," the congruent setting chosen was "home" and the language mix chosen was Spanish
(40) only. In contrast, incongruent factors such as the participants "priest and parishioner" and the setting "beach" yielded less agreement on the third factor of topic and on language choice.

But situational factors do not account for all
(45) code-switching; it occurs even when the domain would lead one not to expect it. In these cases, one language tends to be the primary one, while the other is used only sparingly to achieve certain rhetorical effects. Often the switches are so subtle that the
(50) speakers themselves are not aware of them. This was the case with a study of a family of Puerto Rican Americans in another community. Family members believed they used only English at home, but their taped conversations occasionally contained some
(55) Spanish, with no change in situational factors. When asked what the presence of Spanish signified, they commented that it was used to express certain attitudes such as intimacy or humor more emphatically.

6. Which one of the following most accurately expresses the main point of the passage?

(A) The lives of Puerto Rican Americans are affected in various ways by code-switching.
(B) It is not always possible to explain why code-switching occurs in conversations among Puerto Rican Americans.
(C) Rhetorical factors can explain more instances of code-switching among Puerto Rican Americans than can situational factors.
(D) Studies of bilingual communities of Puerto Rican Americans have caused linguists to revise many of their beliefs about code-switching.
(E) Most code-switching among Puerto Rican Americans can be explained by subtle situational and rhetorical factors.

7. In lines 56–59, the author mentions the family members' explanation of their use of Spanish primarily in order to

(A) report evidence supporting the conclusion that the family's code-switching had a rhetorical basis
(B) show that reasons for code-switching differ from one community to another
(C) supply evidence that seems to conflict with the researchers' conclusions about why the family engaged in code-switching
(D) refute the argument that situational factors explain most code-switching
(E) explain how it could be that the family members failed to notice their use of Spanish

8. Which one of the following questions is NOT characterized by the passage as a question to which linguists sought answers in their code-switching studies involving high school students?

(A) Where do the students involved in the study think that a parent and child are likely to be when they are talking about how to be a good son or daughter?
(B) What language or mix of languages do the students involved in the study think that a parent and child would be likely to use when they are talking at home about how to be a good son or daughter?
(C) What language or mix of languages do the students involved in the study think that a priest and a parishioner would be likely to use if they were conversing on a beach?
(D) What topic do the students involved in the study think that a parent and child would be most likely to discuss when they are speaking Spanish?
(E) What topic do the students involved in the study think that a priest and parishioner would be likely to discuss on a beach?

GO ON TO THE NEXT PAGE.

9. The primary function of the third paragraph of the passage is to

(A) consider a general explanation for the phenomenon of code-switching that is different from the one discussed in the preceding paragraphs

(B) resolve an apparent conflict between two explanations for code-switching that were discussed in the preceding paragraphs

(C) show that there are instances of code-switching that are not explained by the factors discussed in the previous paragraph

(D) report some of the patterns of code-switching observed among a family of Puerto Rican Americans in another community

(E) show that some instances of code-switching are unconscious

10. Based on the passage, which one of the following is best explained as rhetorically determined code-switching?

(A) A speaker who does not know certain words in the primary language of a conversation occasionally has recourse to familiar words in another language.

(B) A person translating a text from one language into another leaves certain words in the original language because the author of the text invented those words.

(C) For the purpose of improved selling strategies, a businessperson who primarily uses one language sometimes conducts business in a second language that is preferred by some people in the community.

(D) A speaker who primarily uses one language switches to another language because it sounds more expressive.

(E) A speaker who primarily uses one language occasionally switches to another language in order to maintain fluency in the secondary language.

11. It can be inferred from the passage that the author would most likely agree with which one of the following statements?

(A) Research revealing that speakers are sometimes unaware of code-switching casts doubt on the results of a prior study involving high school students.

(B) Relevant research conducted prior to the linguists' work with high school students would lead one to expect different answers from those the students actually gave.

(C) Research conducted prior to the study of a family of Puerto Rican Americans was thought by most researchers to explain code-switching in all except the most unusual or nonstandard contexts.

(D) Research suggests that people engaged in code-switching are usually unaware of which situational factors might influence their choice of language or languages.

(E) Research suggests that the family of Puerto Rican Americans does not use code-switching in conversations held at home except for occasional rhetorical effect.

12. Which one of the following does the passage offer as evidence that code-switching cannot be entirely explained by situational factors?

(A) Linguists have observed that bilingual high school students do not agree among themselves as to what mix of languages they would use in the presence of incongruent situational factors.

(B) Code-switching sometimes occurs in conversations whose situational factors would be expected to involve the use of a single language.

(C) Bilingual people often switch smoothly between two languages even when there is no change in the situational context in which the conversation takes place.

(D) Puerto Rican Americans sometimes use Spanish only sparingly and for rhetorical effect in the presence of situational factors that would lead one to expect Spanish to be the primary language.

(E) Speakers who engage in code-switching are often unaware of the situational factors influencing their choices of which language or mix of languages to speak.

13. Which one of the following, if true, would most cast doubt on the author's interpretation of the study involving the family discussed in the third paragraph?

(A) In a previous twelve-month study involving the same family in their home, their conversations were entirely in English except when situational factors changed significantly.

(B) In a subsequent twelve-month study involving the same family, a particular set of situational factors occurred repeatedly without any accompanying instances of code-switching.

(C) In a subsequent twelve-month study involving the same family, it was noted that intimacy and humor were occasionally expressed through the use of English expressions.

(D) When asked about the significance of their use of Spanish, the family members replied in English rather than Spanish.

(E) Prior to their discussions with the researchers, the family members did not describe their occasional use of Spanish as serving to emphasize humor or intimacy.

GO ON TO THE NEXT PAGE.

Reader-response theory, a type of literary theory that arose in reaction to formalist literary criticism, has endeavored to shift the emphasis in the interpretation of literature from the text itself to the
(5) contributions of readers to the meaning of a text. According to literary critics who endorse reader-response theory, the literary text alone renders no meaning; it acquires meaning only when encountered by individual readers, who always bring varying
(10) presuppositions and ways of reading to bear on the text, giving rise to the possibility—even probability—of varying interpretations. This brand of criticism has met opposition from the formalists, who study the text alone and argue that reader-response theory can
(15) encourage and even validate fragmented views of a work, rather than the unified view acquired by examining only the content of the text. However, since no theory has a monopoly on divining meaning from a text, the formalists' view appears
(20) unnecessarily narrow.

The proponents of formalism argue that their approach is firmly grounded in rational, objective principles, while reader-response theory lacks standards and verges on absolute subjectivity. After
(25) all, these proponents argue, no author can create a work that is packed with countless meanings. The meaning of a work of literature, the formalists would argue, may be obscure and somewhat arcane; yet, however hidden it may be, the author's intended
(30) meaning is legible within the work, and it is the critic's responsibility to search closely for this meaning. However, while a literary work is indeed encoded in various signs and symbols that must be translated for the work to be understood and
(35) appreciated, it is not a map. Any complicated literary work will invariably raise more questions than it answers. What is needed is a method that enables the critic to discern and make use of the rich stock of meanings created in encounters between texts and
(40) readers.

Emphasizing the varied presuppositions and perceptions that readers bring to the interpretations of a text can uncover hitherto unnoticed dimensions of the text. In fact, many important works have received
(45) varying interpretations throughout their existence, suggesting that reader-based interpretations similar to those described by reader-response theory had been operating long before the theory's principles were articulated. And while in some cases critics' textual
(50) interpretations based on reader-response theory have unfairly burdened literature of the past with contemporary ideologies, legitimate additional insights and understandings continue to emerge years after an ostensibly definitive interpretation of a major
(55) work has been articulated. By regarding a reader's

personal interpretation of literary works as not only valid but also useful in understanding the works, reader-response theory legitimizes a wide range of perspectives on these works and thereby reinforces
(60) the notion of them as fluid and lively forms of discourse that can continue to support new interpretations long after their original composition.

14. Which one of the following most accurately describes the author's attitude toward formalism as expressed in the passage?

(A) scholarly neutrality
(B) grudging respect
(C) thoughtless disregard
(D) cautious ambivalence
(E) reasoned dismissal

15. Which one of the following persons displays an approach that most strongly suggests sympathy with the principles of reader-response theory?

(A) a translator who translates a poem from Spanish to English word for word so that its original meaning is not distorted
(B) a music critic who insists that early music can be truly appreciated only when it is played on original instruments of the period
(C) a reviewer who finds in the works of a novelist certain unifying themes that reveal the novelist's personal concerns and preoccupations
(D) a folk artist who uses conventional cultural symbols and motifs as a way of conveying commonly understood meanings
(E) a director who sets a play by Shakespeare in nineteenth-century Japan to give a new perspective on the work

16. With which one of the following statements would the author of the passage be most likely to agree?

(A) Any literary theory should be seen ultimately as limiting, since contradictory interpretations of texts are inevitable.
(B) A purpose of a literary theory is to broaden and enhance the understanding that can be gained from a work.
(C) A literary theory should provide valid and strictly objective methods for interpreting texts.
(D) The purpose of a literary theory is to make clear the intended meaning of the author of a work.
(E) Since no literary theory has a monopoly on meaning, a reader should avoid using theories to interpret literature.

GO ON TO THE NEXT PAGE.

17. The passage states that reader-response theory legitimizes which one of the following?

(A) a wide range of perspectives on works of literature
(B) contemporary ideology as a basis for criticism
(C) encoding the meaning of a literary work in signs and symbols
(D) finding the meaning of a work in its text alone
(E) belief that an author's intended meaning in a work is discoverable

18. Which one of the following most accurately describes the author's purpose in referring to literature of the past as being "unfairly burdened" (line 51) in some cases?

(A) to reinforce the notion that reader-based interpretations of texts invariably raise more questions than they can answer
(B) to confirm the longevity of interpretations similar to reader-based interpretations of texts
(C) to point out a fundamental flaw that the author believes makes reader-response theory untenable
(D) to concede a minor weakness in reader-response theory that the author believes is outweighed by its benefits
(E) to suggest that reader-response theory can occasionally encourage fragmented views of a work

19. Which one of the following, if true, most weakens the author's argument concerning reader-response theory?

(A) Reader-response theory is reflected in interpretations that have been given throughout history and that bring additional insight to literary study.
(B) Reader-response theory legitimizes conflicting interpretations that collectively diminish the understanding of a work.
(C) Reader-response theory fails to provide a unified view of the meaning of a literary work.
(D) Reader-response theory claims that a text cannot have meaning without a reader.
(E) Reader-response theory recognizes meanings in a text that were never intended by the author.

20. The author's reference to "various signs and symbols" (line 33) functions primarily to

(A) stress the intricacy and complexity of good literature
(B) grant that a reader must be guided by the text to some degree
(C) imply that no theory alone can fully explain a work of literature
(D) illustrate how a literary work differs from a map
(E) show that an inflexible standard of interpretation provides constant accuracy

21. Which one of the following can most reasonably be inferred from the information in the passage?

(A) Formalists believe that responsible critics who focus on the text alone will tend to find the same or similar meanings in a literary work.
(B) Critical approaches similar to those described by formalism had been used to interpret texts long before the theory was articulated as such.
(C) Formalists would not find any meaning in a text whose author did not intend it to have any one particular meaning.
(D) A literary work from the past can rarely be read properly using reader-response theory when the subtleties of the work's social-historical context are not available.
(E) Formalism is much older and has more adherents than reader-response theory.

GO ON TO THE NEXT PAGE.

Faculty researchers, particularly in scientific, engineering, and medical programs, often produce scientific discoveries and invent products or processes that have potential commercial value. Many
(5) institutions have invested heavily in the administrative infrastructure to develop and exploit these discoveries, and they expect to prosper both by an increased level of research support and by the royalties from licensing those discoveries having
(10) patentable commercial applications. However, although faculty themselves are unlikely to become entrepreneurs, an increasing number of highly valued researchers will be sought and sponsored by research corporations or have consulting contracts with
(15) commercial firms. One study of such entrepreneurship concluded that "if universities do not provide the flexibility needed to venture into business, faculty will be tempted to go to those institutions that are responsive to their commercialized desires." There is
(20) therefore a need to consider the different intellectual property policies that govern the commercial exploitation of faculty inventions in order to determine which would provide the appropriate level of flexibility.
(25) In a recent study of faculty rights, Patricia Chew has suggested a fourfold classification of institutional policies. A supramaximalist institution stakes out the broadest claim possible, asserting ownership not only of all intellectual property produced by faculty in the
(30) course of their employment while using university resources, but also for any inventions or patent rights from faculty activities, even those involving research sponsored by nonuniversity funders. A maximalist institution allows faculty ownership of inventions that
(35) do not arise either "in the course of the faculty's employment [or] from the faculty's use of university resources." This approach, although not as all-encompassing as that of the supramaximalist university, can affect virtually all of a faculty
(40) member's intellectual production. A resource-provider institution asserts a claim to faculty's intellectual product in those cases where "significant use" of university time and facilities is employed. Of course, what constitutes significant use of resources is a
(45) matter of institutional judgment.
As Chew notes, in these policies "faculty rights, including the sharing of royalties, are the result of university benevolence and generosity. [However, this] presumption is contrary to the common law,
(50) which provides that faculty own their inventions." Others have pointed to this anomaly and, indeed, to the uncertain legal and historical basis upon which the ownership of intellectual property rests. Although these issues remain unsettled, and though universities
(55) may be overreaching due to faculty's limited

knowledge of their rights, most major institutions behave in the ways that maximize university ownership and profit participation.
But there is a fourth way, one that seems to be
(60) free from these particular issues. Faculty-oriented institutions assume that researchers own their own intellectual products and the rights to exploit them commercially, except in the development of public health inventions or if there is previously specified
(65) "substantial university involvement." At these institutions industry practice is effectively reversed, with the university benefiting in far fewer circumstances.

22. Which one of the following most accurately summarizes the main point of the passage?

(A) While institutions expect to prosper from increased research support and royalties from patentable products resulting from faculty inventions, if they do not establish clear-cut policies governing ownership of these inventions, they run the risk of losing faculty to research corporations or commercial consulting contracts.

(B) The fourfold classification of institutional policies governing exploitation of faculty inventions is sufficient to categorize the variety of steps institutions are taking to ensure that faculty inventors will not be lured away by commercial firms or research corporations.

(C) To prevent the loss of faculty to commercial firms or research corporations, institutions will have to abandon their insistence on retaining maximum ownership of and profit from faculty inventions and adopt the common-law presumption that faculty alone own their inventions.

(D) While the policies of most institutions governing exploitation of faculty inventions seek to maximize university ownership of and profit from these inventions, another policy offers faculty greater flexibility to pursue their commercial interests by regarding faculty as the owners of their intellectual products.

(E) Most institutional policies governing exploitation of faculty inventions are indefensible because they run counter to common-law notions of ownership and copyright, but they usually go unchallenged because few faculty members are aware of what other options might be available to them.

GO ON TO THE NEXT PAGE.

23. Which one of the following most accurately characterizes the author's view regarding the institutional intellectual property policies of most universities?

  (A) The policies are in keeping with the institution's financial interests.
  (B) The policies are antithetical to the mission of a university.
  (C) The policies do not have a significant impact on the research of faculty.
  (D) The policies are invariably harmful to the motivation of faculty attempting to pursue research projects.
  (E) The policies are illegal and possibly immoral.

24. Which one of the following institutions would NOT be covered by the fourfold classification proposed by Chew?

  (A) an institution in which faculty own the right to some inventions they create outside the institution
  (B) an institution in which faculty own all their inventions, regardless of any circumstances, but grant the institution the right to collect a portion of their royalties
  (C) an institution in which all inventions developed by faculty with institutional resources become the property of the institution
  (D) an institution in which all faculty inventions related to public health become the property of the institution
  (E) an institution in which some faculty inventions created with institutional resources remain the property of the faculty member

25. The passage suggests that the type of institution in which employees are likely to have the most uncertainty about who owns their intellectual products is the

  (A) commercial firm
  (B) supramaximalist university
  (C) maximalist university
  (D) resource-provider university
  (E) faculty-oriented university

26. According to the passage, what distinguishes a resource-provider institution from the other types of institutions identified by Chew is its

  (A) vagueness on the issue of what constitutes university as opposed to nonuniversity resources
  (B) insistence on reaping substantial financial benefit from faculty inventions while still providing faculty with unlimited flexibility
  (C) inversion of the usual practices regarding exploitation of faculty inventions in order to give faculty greater flexibility
  (D) insistence on ownership of faculty inventions developed outside the institution in order to maximize financial benefit to the university
  (E) reliance on the extent of use of institutional resources as the sole criterion in determining ownership of faculty inventions

27. The author of the passage most likely quotes one study of entrepreneurship in lines 16–19 primarily in order to

  (A) explain why institutions may wish to develop intellectual property policies that are responsive to certain faculty needs
  (B) draw a contrast between the worlds of academia and business that will be explored in detail later in the passage
  (C) defend the intellectual property rights of faculty inventors against encroachment by the institutions that employ them
  (D) describe the previous research that led Chew to study institutional policies governing ownership of faculty inventions
  (E) demonstrate that some faculty inventors would be better off working for commercial firms

28. The passage suggests each of the following EXCEPT:

  (A) Supramaximalist institutions run the greatest risk of losing faculty to jobs in institutions more responsive to the inventor's financial interests.
  (B) A faculty-oriented institution will make no claim of ownership to a faculty invention that is unrelated to public health and created without university involvement.
  (C) Faculty at maximalist institutions rarely produce inventions outside the institution without using the institution's resources.
  (D) There is little practical difference between the policies of supramaximalist and maximalist institutions.
  (E) The degree of ownership claimed by a resource-provider institution of the work of its faculty will not vary from case to case.

S T O P

IF YOU FINISH BEFORE TIME IS CALLED, YOU MAY CHECK YOUR WORK ON THIS SECTION ONLY.
DO NOT WORK ON ANY OTHER SECTION IN THE TEST.

SECTION II

Time—35 minutes

25 Questions

Directions: The questions in this section are based on the reasoning contained in brief statements or passages. For some questions, more than one of the choices could conceivably answer the question. However, you are to choose the best answer; that is, the response that most accurately and completely answers the question. You should not make assumptions that are by commonsense standards implausible, superfluous, or incompatible with the passage. After you have chosen the best answer, blacken the corresponding space on your answer sheet.

1. Pettengill: Bebop jazz musicians showed their distaste for jazz classics by taking great liberties with them, as though the songs could be made interesting only through radical reshaping.

   Romney: Only compelling, versatile songs can stand such radical reshaping. Bebop musicians recognized this, and their revolutionary approach to the jazz classics enabled them to discover previously unknown depths in the music.

   Pettengill and Romney disagree over whether

   (A) bebop jazz was radically different from the jazz music that preceded it
   (B) bebop jazz was an improvement on the jazz classics that preceded it
   (C) bebop musicians showed appreciation for jazz classics in radically reshaping them
   (D) jazz music requires musicians to adhere closely to the original version in order to be widely popular
   (E) bebop musicians were influenced by the more conservative styles of their predecessors

2. Essayist: Earth is a living organism, composed of other organisms much as animals are composed of cells, not merely a thing upon which creatures live. This hypothesis is supported by the fact that, like all organisms, Earth can be said to have a metabolism and to regulate its temperature, humidity, and other characteristics, divorced from the influences of its surroundings. Of course, Earth does not literally breathe, but neither do insects (they have no lungs), though they respire successfully.

   The assertion that insects do not literally breathe plays which one of the following roles in the essayist's argument?

   (A) a reason for not rejecting Earth's status as an organism on the basis of its not breathing
   (B) a reason for rejecting as false the belief that Earth is a living organism
   (C) an illustration of the general claim that to be an organism, a creature must have a metabolism
   (D) an example of a type of organism whose status, like Earth's, is unclear
   (E) an illustration of a type of organism out of which Earth is composed

3. Cognitive psychologist: In a recent survey, citizens of Country F were asked to state which one of the following two scenarios they would prefer: (1) Country F is the world economic leader, with a gross national product (GNP) of $100 billion, and Country G is second, with a GNP of $90 billion; or (2) Country G is the economic leader, with a GNP of $120 billion, and Country F is second, with a GNP of $110 billion. Despite the fact that, under scenario 2, Country F would have a higher GNP than under scenario 1, the majority of respondents stated that they preferred scenario 1.

   Which one of the following, if true, would most help to explain the survey results described by the cognitive psychologist?

   (A) Most citizens of Country F believe their country has a higher economic growth rate than Country G.
   (B) Most citizens of Country F want their country to have a GNP higher than $120 billion.
   (C) Most citizens of Country F believe that their personal welfare is unconnected to GNP.
   (D) Most citizens of Country F believe GNP is a poor measure of a nation's economic health.
   (E) Most citizens of Country F want their country to be more economically powerful than Country G.

GO ON TO THE NEXT PAGE.

4. A study claims that the average temperature on Earth has permanently increased, because the average temperature each year for the last five years has been higher than any previous yearly average on record. However, periods of up to ten years of average temperatures that have consistently been record highs are often merely part of the random fluctuations in temperature that are always occurring.

Which one of the following is most strongly supported by the information above?

(A) All large increases in average temperature on record have occurred in ten-year periods.

(B) Five successive years of increasing annual average temperature does not always signify a permanent increase in temperature.

(C) Record high temperatures can be expected on Earth for another five years.

(D) Random fluctuations in Earth's average temperature typically last less than ten years.

(E) The average temperature on Earth never increases except in cases of random temperature fluctuation.

5. Shipping Coordinator: If we send your shipment by air express, it will arrive tomorrow morning. If we send your shipment via ground carrier, it will arrive either tomorrow or the next day. Ground carrier is less expensive than air express, so which do you prefer?

Customer: If I don't choose air express, then I will not receive my shipment tomorrow, so I clearly have no choice but to spend the extra money and have it sent via air express.

The customer's response can best be explained on the assumption that she has misinterpreted the shipping coordinator to mean which one of the following?

(A) Ground carrier is as reliable a shipping method as air express.

(B) If the shipment is sent by air express, it will arrive tomorrow.

(C) Ground carrier is not more expensive than air express.

(D) Unless the shipment is sent by air express, it will not arrive tomorrow.

(E) The greater the shipping cost, the faster the shipment will arrive.

6. Therapists who treat violent criminals cannot both respect their clients' right to confidentiality and be sincerely concerned for the welfare of victims of future violent crimes. Reporting a client's unreported crimes violates the client's trust, but remaining silent leaves the dangerous client out of prison, free to commit more crimes.

Which one of the following, if true, most weakens the argument?

(A) Most therapists who treat violent criminals are assigned this task by a judicial body.

(B) Criminals are no more likely to receive therapy in prison than they are out of prison.

(C) Victims of future violent crimes also have a right to confidentiality should they need therapy.

(D) The right of victims of violent crimes to compensation is as important as the right of criminals in therapy to confidentiality.

(E) A therapist who has gained a violent criminal's trust can persuade that criminal not to commit repeat offenses.

GO ON TO THE NEXT PAGE.

7. Failure to rotate crops depletes the soil's nutrients gradually unless other preventive measures are taken. If the soil's nutrients are completely depleted, additional crops cannot be grown unless fertilizer is applied to the soil. All other things being equal, if vegetables are grown in soil that has had fertilizer applied rather than being grown in non-fertilized soil, they are more vulnerable to pests and, as a consequence, must be treated with larger amounts of pesticides. The more pesticides used on vegetables, the greater the health risks to humans from eating those vegetables.

Suppose there were some vegetables that were grown in soil to which fertilizer had never been applied. On the basis of the passage, which one of the following would have to be true regarding those vegetables?

(A) The soil in which the vegetables were grown may have been completely depleted of nutrients because of an earlier failure to rotate crops.

(B) It is not possible that the vegetables were grown in soil in which crops had been rotated.

(C) The vegetables were grown in soil that had not been completely depleted of nutrients but not necessarily soil in which crops had been rotated.

(D) Whatever the health risks to humans from eating the vegetables, these risks would not be attributable to the use of pesticides on them.

(E) The health risks to humans from eating the vegetables were no less than the health risks to humans from eating the same kinds of vegetables treated with pesticides.

8. Criminologist: Increasing the current prison term for robbery will result in no significant effect in discouraging people from committing robbery.

Each of the following, if true, supports the criminologist's claim EXCEPT:

(A) Many people who rob are motivated primarily by thrill-seeking and risk-taking.

(B) An increase in the prison term for embezzlement did not change the rate at which that crime was committed.

(C) Prison terms for robbery have generally decreased in length recently.

(D) Most people committing robbery believe that they will not get caught.

(E) Most people committing robbery have no idea what the average sentence for robbery is.

9. Activist: As electronic monitoring of employees grows more commonplace and invasive, we hear more and more attempted justifications of this practice by employers. Surveillance, they explain, keeps employees honest, efficient, and polite to customers. Such explanations are obviously self-serving, and so should not be taken to justify these unwarranted invasions of privacy.

A questionable technique used in the activist's argument is to

(A) attack an argument different from that actually offered by the employers

(B) presume that employees are never dishonest, inefficient, or rude

(C) insist that modern business practices meet moral standards far higher than those accepted in the past

(D) attack employers' motives instead of addressing their arguments

(E) make a generalization based on a sample that there is reason to believe is biased

10. When students receive negative criticism generated by computer programs, they are less likely to respond positively than when the critic is a human. Since the acceptance of criticism requires that one respond positively to it, students are more likely to learn from criticism by humans than from criticism by computers.

Which one of the following is an assumption on which the argument depends?

(A) Students are more likely to learn from criticism that they accept than from criticism they do not accept.

(B) Unlike human critics, computers are incapable of showing compassion.

(C) Students always know whether their critics are computers or humans.

(D) Criticism generated by computers is likely to be less favorable than that produced by human critics in response to the same work.

(E) Criticism generated by computers is likely to be no more or less favorable than that produced by human critics in response to the same work.

GO ON TO THE NEXT PAGE.

11. After examining the options, the budget committee discovered that QI's office-phone system would be inexpensive enough to be within the cost limit that had been set for the committee. However, Corelink's system must also be inexpensive enough to be within the limit, since it is even less expensive than QI's system.

The reasoning in the argument above is most closely paralleled by that in which one of the following?

(A) Marissa is just tall enough that she can touch the ceiling when she jumps as high as she can, and since Jeff is taller than Marissa, he too must be able to touch the ceiling when he jumps.

(B) By reducing the number of cigarettes she smoked per day, Kate was able to run five miles, and since Lana smokes fewer cigarettes per day than Kate now does, she too must be able to run five miles.

(C) John's blood-alcohol level was far above the legal limit for driving, so even if it turns out that Paul's blood-alcohol level was lower than John's, it too must have been above the legal limit.

(D) This chocolate is not quite dark enough for it to be the kind that Luis really likes, but that chocolate over there is darker, so it might be just right.

(E) Health Dairy's sharp cheddar cheese is low enough in fat to meet the labeling standard for "low fat" cheddar cheese, and since its mild cheddar cheese is even lower in fat, it too must meet the labeling standard.

12. Essayist: People once believed that Earth was at the center of the universe, and that, therefore, Earth and its inhabitants were important. We now know that Earth revolves around a star at the outskirts of a spiral arm of one of countless galaxies. Therefore, people's old belief that Earth and its inhabitants were important was false.

A flaw in the essayist's argument is that the argument

(A) presumes, without providing justification, that only true statements can have good reasons to be believed

(B) neglects to consider that a statement that was believed for questionable reasons may nevertheless have been true

(C) fails to consider that there can be no reason for disbelieving a true statement

(D) overlooks the fact that people's perception of their importance changed from century to century

(E) neglects the fact that people's perception of their importance varies from culture to culture

13. Davis: The only relevant factor in determining appropriate compensation for property damage or theft is the value the property loses due to damage or the value of the property stolen; the harm to the victim is directly proportional to the pertinent value.

Higuchi: I disagree. More than one factor must be considered: A victim who recovers the use of personal property after two years is owed more than a victim who recovers its use after only one year.

Davis's and Higuchi's statements most strongly support the view that they would disagree with each other about which one of the following?

(A) It is possible to consistently and reliably determine the amount of compensation owed to someone whose property was damaged or stolen.

(B) Some victims are owed increased compensation because of the greater dollar value of the damage done to their property.

(C) Victims who are deprived of their property are owed compensation in proportion to the harm they have suffered.

(D) Some victims are owed increased compensation because of the greater amount of time they are deprived of the use of their property.

(E) The compensation owed to victims should be determined on a case-by-case basis rather than by some general rule.

14. Resident: Residents of this locale should not consider their loss of farming as a way of life to be a tragedy. When this area was a rural area it was economically depressed, but it is now a growing bastion of high-tech industry with high-wage jobs, and supports over 20 times the number of jobs it did then.

Which one of the following, if true, does the most to justify the conclusion of the resident's argument?

(A) Farming is becoming increasingly efficient, with the result that fewer farms are required to produce the same amount of food.

(B) The development of high-tech industry is more valuable to national security than is farming.

(C) Residents of this locale do not value a rural way of life more than they value economic prosperity.

(D) Many residents of this locale have annual incomes that are twice what they were when the locale was primarily agricultural.

(E) The loss of a family farm is often perceived as tragic even when no financial hardship results.

15. Kendrick: Governments that try to prevent cigarettes from being advertised are justified in doing so, since such advertisements encourage people to engage in an unhealthy practice. But cigarette advertisements should remain legal since advertisements for fatty foods are legal, even though those advertisements also encourage people to engage in unhealthy practices.

Which one of the following, if true, most helps to resolve the apparent conflict between Kendrick's statements?

(A) Any advertisement that encourages people to engage in an unhealthy practice should be made illegal, even though the legality of some such advertisements is currently uncontroversial.

(B) The advertisement of fattening foods, unlike that of cigarettes, should not be prevented, because fattening foods, unlike cigarettes, are not addictive.

(C) Most advertisements should be legal, although advertisers are always morally responsible for ensuring that their advertisements do not encourage people to engage in unhealthy practices.

(D) Governments should try to prevent the advertisement of cigarettes by means of financial disincentives rather than by legal prohibition.

(E) Governments should place restrictions on cigarette advertisements so as to keep them from encouraging people to engage in unhealthy practices, but should not try to prevent such advertisements.

16. Environmentalist: Many people prefer to live in regions of natural beauty. Such regions often experience an influx of new residents, and a growing population encourages businesses to relocate to those regions. Thus, governmentally mandated environmental protection in regions of natural beauty can help those regions' economies overall, even if such protection harms some older local industries.

Which one of the following is an assumption on which the environmentalist's argument depends?

(A) Regions of natural beauty typically are beautiful enough to attract new residents only until governmentally mandated environmental protection that damages local industries is imposed.

(B) The economies of most regions of natural beauty are not based primarily on local industries that would be harmed by governmentally mandated environmental protection.

(C) If governmentally mandated environmental protection helps a region's economy, it does so primarily by encouraging people to move into that region.

(D) Voluntary environmental protection usually does not help a region's economy to the degree that governmentally mandated protection does.

(E) A factor harmful to some older local industries in a region need not discourage other businesses from relocating to that region.

GO ON TO THE NEXT PAGE.

17. No small countries and no countries in the southern hemisphere have permanent seats on the United Nations Security Council. Each of the five countries with a permanent seat on the Security Council is in favor of increased international peacekeeping efforts and a greater role for the United Nations in moderating regional disputes. However, some countries that are in favor of increased international peacekeeping efforts are firmly against increased spending on refugees by the United Nations.

If the statements above are true, which one of the following must also be true?

(A) Some small countries do not want the United Nations to increase its spending on refugees.
(B) Some countries in the southern hemisphere are not in favor of increased international peacekeeping efforts.
(C) Some countries that have permanent seats on the United Nations Security Council are against increased spending on refugees by the United Nations.
(D) Some small countries are in favor of a greater role for the United Nations in moderating regional disputes.
(E) Some countries that are in favor of a greater role for the United Nations in moderating regional disputes are not located in the southern hemisphere.

18. Editorial: It is clear that what is called "health education" is usually propaganda rather than education. Propaganda and education are never the same thing. The former is nothing but an attempt to influence behavior through the repetition of simplistic slogans, whereas the latter never involves such a method. Though education does attempt to influence behavior, it does so by offering information in all its complexity, leaving it up to the individual to decide how to act on that information. Sadly, however, propaganda is much more successful than education.

The conclusion drawn by the editorial follows logically if it is assumed that what is called "health education" usually

(A) does not leave it up to the individual to decide how to act on information
(B) does not offer information in all its complexity
(C) does not involve the repetition of simplistic slogans
(D) attempts to influence behavior solely by repeating simplistic slogans
(E) is very successful in influencing people's behavior

19. Marc: The fact that the people of our country look back on the past with a great deal of nostalgia demonstrates that they regret the recent revolution.

Robert: They are not nostalgic for the recent past, but for the distant past, which the prerevolutionary regime despised; this indicates that although they are troubled, they do not regret the revolution.

Their dialogue provides the most support for the claim that Marc and Robert agree that the people of their country

(A) tend to underrate past problems when the country faces troubling times
(B) are looking to the past for solutions to the country's current problems
(C) are likely to repeat former mistakes if they look to the country's past for solutions to current problems
(D) are concerned about the country's current situation and this is evidenced by their nostalgia
(E) tend to be most nostalgic for the things that are the farthest in their past

20. Social critic: One of the most important ways in which a society socializes children is by making them feel ashamed of their immoral behavior. But in many people this shame results in deep feelings of guilt and self-loathing that can be a severe hardship. Thus, moral socialization has had a net effect of increasing the total amount of suffering.

The social critic's argument is most vulnerable to criticism on the grounds that it

(A) overlooks the possibility that the purported source of a problem could be modified to avoid that problem without being eliminated altogether
(B) fails to address adequately the possibility that one phenomenon may causally contribute to the occurrence of another, even though the two phenomena do not always occur together
(C) presumes, without providing justification, that a phenomenon that supposedly increases the total amount of suffering in a society should therefore be changed or eliminated, regardless of its beneficial consequences
(D) takes for granted that a behavior that sometimes leads to a certain phenomenon cannot also significantly reduce the overall occurrence of that phenomenon
(E) presumes, without providing justification, that if many people have a negative psychological reaction to a phenomenon, then no one can have a positive reaction to that phenomenon

21. Curator: A magazine recently ran a very misleading story on the reaction of local residents to our controversial art exhibit. They quoted the responses of three residents, all of whom expressed a sense of moral outrage. These quotations were intended to suggest that most local residents oppose the exhibit; the story failed to mention, however, the fact that the three residents are all close friends.

Which one of the following principles most helps to justify the curator's argumentation?

(A) It is misleading to present the opinions of people with no special expertise on a subject as though they were experts.

(B) It is misleading to present the opinions of people on only one side of an issue when the population is likely to be evenly divided on that issue.

(C) It is misleading to present the opinions of a few people as evidence of what the majority thinks unless the opinions they express are widely held.

(D) It is misleading to present testimony from close friends and thereby imply that they must agree with each other.

(E) It is misleading to present the opinions of a potentially nonrepresentative sample of people as if they represent public opinion.

22. All parrots can learn to speak a few words and phrases. Not all parrots have equally pleasant dispositions, though some of those native to Australia can be counted on for a sweet temper. Almost any parrot, however, will show tremendous affection for an owner who raised the bird from a chick by hand-feeding it.

If the statements above are true, then which one of the following must be true?

(A) Some parrots that can learn to speak are sweet tempered.

(B) If a parrot is not native to Australia, then it will be sweet tempered only if it is hand-fed as a chick.

(C) The sweetest-tempered parrots are those native to Australia.

(D) Australia is the only place where one can find birds that can both learn to speak and be relied on for a sweet temper.

(E) All species of pet birds that are native to Australia can be counted on for a sweet temper.

23. Toxicologist: Recent research has shown that dioxin causes cancer in rats. Although similar research has never been done on humans, and probably never will be, the use of dioxin should be completely banned.

That dioxin causes cancer in rats figures in the argument in which one of the following ways?

(A) It is presented as the hazard that the researcher is concerned with preventing.

(B) It is presented as a benefit of not acting on the recommendation in the conclusion.

(C) It is presented as evidence for the claim that similar research will never be done on humans.

(D) It is presented as a finding that motivates the course of action advocated in the conclusion.

(E) It is presented as evidence for the claim that similar research has never been done on humans.

GO ON TO THE NEXT PAGE.

24. Politician: The law should not require people to wear seat belts in cars. People are allowed to ride motorcycles without seat belts, and riding a motorcycle even while wearing a seat belt would be more dangerous than riding in a car without wearing one.

Which one of the following arguments is most similar in its flawed reasoning to the politician's argument?

(A) Marielle and Pat should allow their children to have snacks between meals. They currently allow their children to have a large dessert after dinner, and allowing them to have snacks between meals instead would improve their nutrition.

(B) Any corporation should allow its employees to take time off when they are under too much stress to concentrate on their work. Some corporations allow any employee with a bad cold to take time off, and even a healthy employee under stress may be less productive than an unstressed employee with a bad cold.

(C) Amusement parks should allow people to stand while riding roller coasters. It is legal for people to stand at the edges of high cliffs, and even sitting at the edge of a high cliff is more likely to result in a fatal fall than standing while riding a roller coaster.

(D) It should be illegal for anyone to smoke in a public place, for it certainly should be illegal to pollute public drinking water, and smoking even in the privacy of one's home can be more harmful to the health of others than polluting their water would be.

(E) Vanessa should be allowed to let her dog run around in the park without a leash. She already lets the dog roam around her yard without a leash, and the park differs from her yard only in size.

25. Burying beetles do whatever they can to minimize the size of their competitors' broods without adversely affecting their own. This is why they routinely destroy each other's eggs when two or more beetles inhabit the same breeding location. Yet, after the eggs hatch, the adults treat all of the larvae equally, sharing in the care of the entire population.

Which one of the following, if true, most helps to explain burying beetles' apparently contradictory behavior?

(A) Burying beetles whose eggs hatch before their competitors' are more likely to have large broods than are burying beetles whose eggs hatch later.

(B) The cooperation among adult burying beetles ensures that the greatest possible number of larvae survive.

(C) Burying beetles are unable to discriminate between their own larvae and the larvae of other burying beetles.

(D) Many of the natural enemies of burying beetles can be repelled only if burying beetles cooperate in defending the breeding site.

(E) Most breeding sites for burying beetles can accommodate only a limited number of larvae.

S T O P

IF YOU FINISH BEFORE TIME IS CALLED, YOU MAY CHECK YOUR WORK ON THIS SECTION ONLY.
DO NOT WORK ON ANY OTHER SECTION IN THE TEST.

SECTION III

Time—35 minutes

26 Questions

<u>Directions:</u>   The questions in this section are based on the reasoning contained in brief statements or passages. For some questions, more than one of the choices could conceivably answer the question. However, you are to choose the <u>best</u> answer; that is, the response that most accurately and completely answers the question. You should not make assumptions that are by commonsense standards implausible, superfluous, or incompatible with the passage. After you have chosen the best answer, blacken the corresponding space on your answer sheet.

1. The development of new inventions is promoted by the granting of patent rights, which restrict the right of anyone but the patent holders to profit from these inventions for a specified period. Without patent rights, anyone could simply copy another's invention; consequently, inventors would have no financial incentive for investing the time and energy required to develop new products. Thus, it is important to continue to grant patent rights, or else no one will engage in original development and consequently no new inventions will be forthcoming.

   Which one of the following is an assumption on which the argument depends?

   (A)   Financial reward is the only incentive that will be effective in motivating people to develop new inventions.

   (B)   When an inventor sells patent rights to a manufacturer, the manufacturer makes less total profit on the invention than the inventor does.

   (C)   Any costs incurred by a typical inventor in applying for patent rights are insignificant in comparison to the financial benefit of holding the patent rights.

   (D)   Patent rights should be granted only if an inventor's product is not similar to another invention already covered by patent rights.

   (E)   The length of a patent right is usually proportional to the costs involved in inventing the product.

2. The Fenwicks returned home from a trip to find two broken bottles on their kitchen floor. There was no sign of forced entry and nothing in the house appeared to have been taken. Although the Fenwicks have a pet cat that had free run of the house while they were away, the Fenwicks hypothesized that they had left a back door unlocked and that neighborhood children had entered through it, attempted to raid the kitchen, and left after breaking the bottles.

   Each of the following, if true, helps to support the Fenwicks' hypothesis EXCEPT:

   (A)   A neighbor thought he had seen the Fenwicks' back door closing while the Fenwicks were away.

   (B)   When the Fenwicks returned home, they found children's footprints on the back porch that had not been there before their trip.

   (C)   The two bottles that the Fenwicks found broken on their kitchen floor had been in the refrigerator when the Fenwicks left on vacation.

   (D)   There have been several recent burglaries in the Fenwicks' neighborhood in which neighborhood children were suspected.

   (E)   The Fenwicks returned home from their trip later than they had planned.

GO ON TO THE NEXT PAGE.

3. In an experiment, tennis players who were told that their performance would be used to assess only the quality of their rackets performed much better than an equally skilled group of tennis players who were told that their tennis-playing talent would be measured.

The situation described above most closely conforms to which one of the following propositions?

(A) People do less well on a task if they have been told that they will be closely watched while doing it.

(B) People execute a task more proficiently when they do not believe their abilities are being judged.

(C) People perform a task more proficiently when they have confidence in their abilities.

(D) People who assess their talents accurately generally perform near their actual level of proficiency.

(E) People who think that a superior performance will please those who are testing them generally try harder.

4. Sydonie: Parents differ in their beliefs about the rules to which their children should be subject. So any disciplinary structure in schools is bound to create resentment because it will contradict some parental approaches to raising children.

Stephanie: Your conclusion is incorrect; educational research shows that when parents list the things that they most want their children's schools to provide, good discipline is always high on the list.

Stephanie's argument is most vulnerable to criticism on the grounds that

(A) it focuses on educational research rather than educational practice

(B) it addresses a more general issue than that addressed in Sydonie's argument

(C) it does not counter Sydonie's suggestion that parents have diverse ideas of what constitutes good discipline

(D) the phrase "high on the list" is not specific enough to give useful information about what parents desire from a school

(E) it fails to discuss educators' attitudes toward discipline in schools

5. Art critic: The aesthetic value of a work of art lies in its ability to impart a stimulating character to the audience's experience of the work.

Which one of the following judgments most closely conforms with the principle cited above?

(A) This painting is aesthetically deficient because it is an exact copy of a painting done 30 years ago.

(B) This symphony is beautiful because, even though it does not excite the audience, it is competently performed.

(C) This sculpted four-inch cube is beautiful because it is carved from material which, although much like marble, is very rare.

(D) This painting is aesthetically valuable because it was painted by a highly controversial artist.

(E) This poem is aesthetically deficient because it has little impact on its audience.

6. Antonia: The stock market is the best place to invest your money these days; although it is often volatile, it provides the opportunity to make a large profit quickly.

Maria: I agree that the stock market provides the opportunity to make large profits quickly, but one is just as likely to take a huge loss. I think it is better to invest in savings bonds, which provide a constant, reliable income over many years.

Antonia's and Maria's statements provide the most support for holding that they disagree about whether

(A) the stock market is often volatile but provides the opportunity to make a large profit quickly

(B) savings bonds can provide a large return on one's investment

(C) the stock market provides the opportunity for an investor to make a constant, reliable income over many years

(D) it is safer to invest in savings bonds than to invest in the stock market

(E) it is preferable to pick an investment offering a reliable income over a riskier opportunity to make a large profit quickly

GO ON TO THE NEXT PAGE.

7. Very little is known about prehistoric hominid cave dwellers. However, a recent study of skeletons of these hominids has revealed an important clue about their daily activities: skeletal fractures present are most like the type and distribution of fractures sustained by rodeo riders. Therefore, it is likely that these cave dwellers engaged in activities similar to rodeo riders—chasing and tackling animals.

Which one of the following principles, if valid, most helps to justify the argumentation above?

(A) The primary source of clues about the lives of prehistoric hominids is their skeletal remains.

(B) The most important aspect of prehistoric life to be studied is how food was obtained.

(C) If direct evidence as to the cause of a phenomenon is available, then indirect evidence should not be sought.

(D) If there is a similarity between two effects, then there is probably a similarity between their causes.

(E) The frequency with which a hazardous activity is performed is proportional to the frequency of injuries resulting from that activity.

8. Studies suggest that, for the vast majority of people who have normal blood pressure, any amount of sodium greater than that required by the body is simply excreted and does not significantly raise blood pressure. So only persons who have high blood pressure and whose bodies are incapable of safely processing excess sodium need to restrict their sodium intake.

Which one of the following, if true, would most seriously weaken the argument?

(A) High blood pressure is more harmful than was previously believed.

(B) High blood pressure is sometimes exacerbated by intake of more sodium than the body requires.

(C) Excess sodium intake over time often destroys the body's ability to process excess sodium.

(D) Every human being has a physiological need for at least some sodium.

(E) Any sodium not used by the body will increase blood pressure unless it is excreted.

9. Most lecturers who are effective teachers are eccentric, but some noneccentric lecturers are very effective teachers. In addition, every effective teacher is a good communicator.

Which one of the following statements follows logically from the statements above?

(A) Some good communicators are eccentric.

(B) All good communicators are effective teachers.

(C) Some lecturers who are not effective teachers are not eccentric.

(D) Most lecturers who are good communicators are eccentric.

(E) Some noneccentric lecturers are effective teachers but are not good communicators.

10. Recently, photons and neutrinos emitted by a distant supernova, an explosion of a star, reached Earth at virtually the same time. This finding supports Einstein's claim that gravity is a property of space itself, in the sense that a body exerts gravitational pull by curving the space around it. The simultaneous arrival of the photons and neutrinos is evidence that the space through which they traveled was curved.

Which one of the following, if true, would most strengthen the reasoning above?

(A) Einstein predicted that photons and neutrinos emitted by any one supernova would reach Earth simultaneously.

(B) If gravity is not a property of space itself, then photons and neutrinos emitted simultaneously by a distant event will reach Earth at different times.

(C) Photons and neutrinos emitted by distant events would be undetectable on Earth if Einstein's claim that gravity is a property of space itself were correct.

(D) Photons and neutrinos were the only kinds of particles that reached Earth from the supernova.

(E) Prior to the simultaneous arrival of photons and neutrinos from the supernova, there was no empirical evidence for Einstein's claim that gravity is a property of space itself.

GO ON TO THE NEXT PAGE.

11. Geneticist: Billions of dollars are spent each year on high-profile experiments that attempt to link particular human genes with particular personality traits. Though such experiments seem to promise a new understanding of human nature, they have few practical consequences. Meanwhile, more mundane and practical genetic projects—for example, those that look for natural ways to make edible plants hardier or more nutritious—are grossly underfunded. Thus, funding for human gene research should be reduced while funding for other genetic research should be increased.

Which one of the following principles, if valid, most helps to justify the geneticist's reasoning?

(A) Experiments that have the potential to help the whole human race are more worthwhile than those that help only a small number of people.

(B) Experiments that focus on the genetics of plants are more practical than those that focus on the genetics of human nature.

(C) Experiments that help prevent malnutrition are more worthwhile than those that help prevent merely undesirable personality traits.

(D) Experiments that have modest but practical goals are more worthwhile than those that have impressive goals but few practical consequences.

(E) Experiments that get little media attention and are not widely supported by the public are more valuable than are those that get much media coverage and have wide public support.

12. Some argue that because attaining governmental power in democracies requires building majority coalitions, it is a necessary evil that policymakers do not adhere rigorously to principle when dealing with important issues, but rather shift policies as they try to please different constituents at different times. But it is precisely this behavior that allows a democracy to adapt more easily to serve public interests, and thus it is more a benefit than an evil.

Which one of the following is an assumption required by the argument?

(A) Government policymakers cannot retain power if they ignore any of the various factions of their original winning coalition.

(B) Democracies are more likely than nondemocratic forms of government to have policymakers who understand the complexity of governmental issues.

(C) In the formulation of government policy, the advantage conferred by adaptability to diverse or fluctuating public interests outweighs the detriment associated with a lack of strict fidelity to principle.

(D) In dealing with an important issue, policymakers in a democracy appeal to a principle in dealing with an issue only when that principle has majority support.

(E) Democracies appear to be more flexible than nondemocratic forms of government, but are not actually so.

GO ON TO THE NEXT PAGE.

13. Up until about 2 billion years ago, the sun was 30 percent dimmer than it is now. If the sun were that dim now, our oceans would be completely frozen. According to fossil evidence, however, life and liquid water were both present as early as 3.8 billion years ago.

Which one of the following, if true, most helps to resolve the apparent discrepancy described above?

(A) Our atmosphere currently holds in significantly less heat than it did 3.8 billion years ago.
(B) The liquid water present 3.8 billion years ago later froze, only to melt again about 2 billion years ago.
(C) A significant source of heat other than the sun contributed to the melting of ice sheets approximately 2 billion years ago.
(D) Evidence suggests that certain regions of ocean remained frozen until much more recently than 2 billion years ago.
(E) When large portions of the globe are ice-covered, more of the sun's heat is reflected and not absorbed by the earth than when only the poles are ice-covered.

14. Social critic: The operas composed by Bizet and Verdi are nineteenth-century European creations, reflecting the attitudes and values in France and Italy at the end of that century. Several recent studies impugn these operas on the grounds that they reinforce in our society many stereotypes about women. But only a small minority of contemporary North Americans, namely opera lovers, have had any significant exposure to these works.

Which one of the following most accurately expresses the conclusion that the social critic's argument, as it is stated above, is structured to establish?

(A) Bizet and Verdi constructed images of women that have significantly influenced contemporary stereotypes.
(B) Nineteenth-century French and Italian images of women are quite different from contemporary North American images of women.
(C) The operas of Bizet and Verdi have not significantly contributed to stereotypical images of women in contemporary North America.
(D) Opera is not an important factor shaping social attitudes in contemporary North America.
(E) People cannot be influenced by things they are not directly exposed to.

15. In 1975, a province reduced its personal income tax rate by 2 percent for most taxpayers. In 1976, the personal income tax rate for those taxpayers was again reduced by 2 percent. Despite the decreases in the personal income tax rate, the total amount of money collected from personal income taxes remained constant from 1974 to 1975 and rose substantially in 1976.

Each of the following, if true, could help to resolve the apparent discrepancy described above EXCEPT:

(A) The years 1975 and 1976 were ones in which the province's economy was especially prosperous.
(B) The definition of "personal income" used by the province was widened during 1975 to include income received from personal investments.
(C) The personal income tax rate for the wealthiest individuals in the province rose during 1975 and 1976.
(D) The province's total revenue from all taxes increased during both 1975 and 1976.
(E) A large number of people from other provinces moved to the province during 1975 and 1976.

16. Everything that is commonplace and ordinary fails to catch our attention, so there are things that fail to catch our attention but that are miracles of nature.

The conclusion of the argument follows logically if which one of the following is assumed?

(A) Only miracles of nature fail to be ordinary and commonplace.
(B) Some things that are ordinary and commonplace are miracles of nature.
(C) Some things that are commonplace and ordinary fail to catch our attention.
(D) Everything that fails to catch our attention is commonplace and ordinary.
(E) Only extraordinary or unusual things catch our attention.

GO ON TO THE NEXT PAGE.

17. If one of the effects of a genetic mutation makes a substantial contribution to the survival of the species, then, and only then, will that mutation be favored in natural selection. This process is subject to one proviso, namely that the traits that were not favored, yet were carried along by a trait that was favored, must not be so negative as to annul the benefits of having the new, favored trait.

If the statements above are true, each of the following could be true EXCEPT:

(A) A species possesses a trait whose effects are all neutral for the survival of that species.
(B) All the effects of some genetic mutations contribute substantially to the survival of a species.
(C) A species possesses a trait that reduces the species' survival potential.
(D) A genetic mutation that carries along several negative traits is favored in natural selection.
(E) A genetic mutation whose effects are all neutral to a species is favored in natural selection.

18. In a highly publicized kidnapping case in Ontario, the judge barred all media and spectators from the courtroom. Her decision was based on the judgment that the public interest would not be served by allowing spectators. A local citizen argued, "They pleaded with the public to help find the victim; they pleaded with the public to provide tips; they aroused the public interest, then they claimed that allowing us to attend would not serve the public interest. These actions are inconsistent."

The reasoning in the local citizen's argument is flawed because this argument

(A) generalizes from an atypical case
(B) trades on an ambiguity with respect to the term "public interest"
(C) overlooks the fact that the judge might not be the one who made the plea to the public for help
(D) attempts to support its conclusion by making sensationalistic appeals
(E) presumes that the public's right to know is obviously more important than the defendant's right to a fair trial

19. Today's farmers plant only a handful of different strains of a given crop. Crops lack the diversity that they had only a few generations ago. Hence, a disease that strikes only a few strains of crops, and that would have had only minor impact on the food supply in the past, would devastate it today.

Which one of the following, if true, would most weaken the argument?

(A) In the past, crop diseases would often devastate food supplies throughout entire regions.
(B) Affected crops can quickly be replaced from seed banks that store many strains of those crops.
(C) Some of the less popular seed strains that were used in the past were more resistant to many diseases than are the strains popular today.
(D) Humans today have more variety in their diets than in the past, but still rely heavily on cereal crops like rice and wheat.
(E) Today's crops are much less vulnerable to damage from insects or encroachment by weeds than were crops of a few generations ago.

20. Interviewer: A certain company released a model of computer whose microprocessor design was flawed, making that computer liable to process information incorrectly. How did this happen?

Industry spokesperson: Given the huge number of circuits in the microprocessor of any modern computer, not every circuit can be manually checked before a computer model that contains the microprocessor is released.

Interviewer: Then what guarantee do we have that new microprocessors will not be similarly flawed?

Industry spokesperson: There is no chance of further microprocessor design flaws, since all microprocessors are now entirely computer-designed.

The industry spokesperson's argument is most vulnerable to criticism on the grounds that it

(A) presumes, without providing justification, that the microprocessor quality-control procedures of the company mentioned are not representative of those followed throughout the industry
(B) ignores the possibility that a microprocessor can have a flaw other than a design flaw
(C) overlooks the possibility that a new computer model is liable to malfunction for reasons other than a microprocessor flaw
(D) treats a single instance of a microprocessor design flaw as evidence that there will be many such flaws
(E) takes for granted, despite evidence to the contrary, that some computers are not liable to error

GO ON TO THE NEXT PAGE.

21. Each of the many people who participated in the town's annual spring cleanup received a community recognition certificate. Because the spring cleanup took place at the same time as the downtown arts fair, we know that there are at least some spring cleanup participants who are not active in the town's artistic circles.

If the statements above are true, which one of the following must be true?

(A) Some of the persons who are active in the town's artistic circles received community recognition certificates.
(B) Not all of those who received community recognition certificates are active in the town's artistic circles.
(C) No participants in the downtown arts fair received community recognition certificates.
(D) No person who received a community recognition certificate has not participated in the spring cleanup.
(E) Persons who are active in the town's artistic circles are not concerned with the town's environment.

22. Taking advanced mathematics courses should increase a student's grade point average, for, as numerous studies have shown, students who have taken one or more advanced mathematics courses are far more likely to have high grade point averages than students who have not taken such courses.

The flawed pattern of reasoning in the argument above is most similar to that in which one of the following?

(A) Fur color is in large measure hereditary, for, as many studies have shown, black cats are more likely than others to have black kittens, and orange cats are more likely to have orange kittens.
(B) Water can cause intoxication. After all, imbibing scotch and water, whiskey and water, bourbon and water, gin and water, and vodka and water all cause intoxication.
(C) Eating a diet consisting primarily of fats and carbohydrates may cause weight gain in some people. Studies have shown that many overweight people eat such diets.
(D) Buying running shoes should increase the frequency with which a person exercises, since those who buy two or more pairs of running shoes each year tend to exercise more often than those who buy at most one pair.
(E) Reading to children at an early age should inspire them to read on their own later, since studies have shown that children who have not been read to are less likely to develop an interest in reading than children who have been read to.

23. Each of many different human hormones can by itself raise the concentration of glucose in the blood. The reason for this is probably a metabolic quirk of the brain. To see this, consider that although most human cells can produce energy from fats and proteins, brain cells can use only glucose. Thus, if blood glucose levels fall too low, brain cells will rapidly starve, leading to unconsciousness and death.

Which one of the following most accurately expresses the main conclusion of the argument above?

(A) Each of many different human hormones can by itself raise blood glucose levels.
(B) The reason that many different hormones can each independently raise blood glucose levels is probably a metabolic quirk of the brain.
(C) Although most human cells can produce energy from fats and proteins, brain cells can produce energy only from glucose.
(D) If blood glucose levels fall too low, then brain cells starve, resulting in loss of consciousness and death.
(E) The reason brain cells starve if deprived of glucose is that they can produce energy only from glucose.

24. Human resources director: While only some recent university graduates consider work environment an important factor in choosing a job, they all consider salary an important factor. Further, whereas the only workers who consider stress level an important factor in choosing a job are a few veteran employees, every recent university graduate considers vacation policy an important factor.

If all of the statements of the human resources director are true, then which one of the following must be true?

(A) All people who consider work environment an important factor in choosing a job also consider salary an important factor.
(B) At least some people who consider work environment an important factor in choosing a job consider vacation policy an important factor as well.
(C) At least some veteran employees do not consider work environment an important factor in choosing a job.
(D) All people who consider vacation policy an important factor in choosing a job also consider salary an important factor.
(E) No one for whom salary is an important factor in choosing a job also considers stress level an important factor.

GO ON TO THE NEXT PAGE.

25. Wealth is not a good thing, for good things cause no harm at all, yet wealth is often harmful to people.

Which one of the following arguments is most similar in its pattern of reasoning to the argument above?

(A) Alex loves to golf, and no one in the chess club loves to golf. It follows that Alex is not in the chess club.

(B) Isabella must be a contented baby. She smiles a great deal and hardly ever cries, like all happy people.

(C) Growth in industry is not a good thing for our town. Although the economy might improve, the pollution would be unbearable.

(D) Sarah's dog is not a dachshund, for he hunts very well, and most dachshunds hunt poorly.

(E) There is usually more traffic at this time of day, unless it is a holiday. But since today is not a holiday, it is surprising that there is so little traffic.

26. In the aftermath of the Cold War, international relations between Cold War allies became more difficult. Leaders of previously allied nations were required to conduct tactful economic negotiations in order not to arouse tensions that had previously been overlooked.

The situation described above conforms most closely to which one of the following propositions?

(A) International economic competition is a greater cause of tension than is international military competition.

(B) Bonds between allies are stronger when they derive from fear of a common enemy than when they derive from common economic goals.

(C) When there is a military commitment between countries, fundamental agreement between them on economic matters is more easily reached.

(D) Economic matters are considered unimportant during periods of actual or threatened war.

(E) A common enemy contributes to a strengthened bond between nations, enabling them to ignore economic tensions that would otherwise be problematic.

S T O P

IF YOU FINISH BEFORE TIME IS CALLED, YOU MAY CHECK YOUR WORK ON THIS SECTION ONLY.
DO NOT WORK ON ANY OTHER SECTION IN THE TEST.

SECTION IV

Time—35 minutes

22 Questions

Directions: Each group of questions in this section is based on a set of conditions. In answering some of the questions, it may be useful to draw a rough diagram. Choose the response that most accurately and completely answers each question and blacken the corresponding space on your answer sheet.

Questions 1–5

There are exactly six groups in this year's Civic Parade: firefighters, gymnasts, jugglers, musicians, puppeteers, and veterans. Each group marches as a unit; the groups are ordered from first, at the front of the parade, to sixth, at the back. The following conditions apply:

At least two groups march behind the puppeteers but ahead of the musicians.

Exactly one group marches behind the firefighters but ahead of the veterans.

The gymnasts are the first, third, or fifth group.

1. Which one of the following could be an accurate list of the groups in the Civic Parade in order from first to last?

   (A) firefighters, puppeteers, veterans, musicians, gymnasts, jugglers
   (B) gymnasts, puppeteers, jugglers, musicians, firefighters, veterans
   (C) veterans, puppeteers, firefighters, gymnasts, jugglers, musicians
   (D) jugglers, puppeteers, gymnasts, firefighters, musicians, veterans
   (E) musicians, veterans, jugglers, firefighters, gymnasts, puppeteers

2. If the gymnasts march immediately ahead of the veterans, then which one of the following could be the fourth group?

   (A) gymnasts
   (B) jugglers
   (C) musicians
   (D) puppeteers
   (E) veterans

3. If the veterans march immediately behind the puppeteers, then which one of the following could be the second group?

   (A) firefighters
   (B) gymnasts
   (C) jugglers
   (D) musicians
   (E) veterans

4. If the jugglers are the fifth group, then which one of the following must be true?

   (A) The puppeteers are the first group.
   (B) The firefighters are the first group.
   (C) The veterans are the second group.
   (D) The gymnasts are the third group.
   (E) The musicians are the sixth group.

5. Which one of the following groups CANNOT march immediately behind the gymnasts?

   (A) firefighters
   (B) jugglers
   (C) musicians
   (D) puppeteers
   (E) veterans

GO ON TO THE NEXT PAGE.

Questions 6–12

A rowing team uses a boat with exactly six seats arranged in single file and numbered sequentially 1 through 6, from the front of the boat to the back. Six athletes—Lee, Miller, Ovitz, Singh, Valerio, and Zita—each row at exactly one of the seats. The following restrictions must apply:

Miller rows closer to the front than Singh.
Singh rows closer to the front than both Lee and Valerio.
Valerio and Zita each row closer to the front than Ovitz.

6. Which one of the following could be an accurate matching of athletes to seats?

(A) Miller: seat 1; Valerio: seat 5; Lee: seat 6
(B) Singh: seat 3; Valerio: seat 4; Zita: seat 5
(C) Miller: seat 1; Valerio: seat 3; Lee: seat 6
(D) Lee: seat 3; Valerio: seat 4; Ovitz: seat 5
(E) Zita: seat 2; Valerio: seat 3; Ovitz: seat 6

7. If Valerio rows at seat 5, then which one of the following must be true?

(A) Miller rows at seat 1.
(B) Singh rows at seat 2.
(C) Zita rows at seat 3.
(D) Lee rows at seat 4.
(E) Ovitz rows at seat 6.

8. If Lee rows at seat 3, then each of the following could be true EXCEPT:

(A) Zita rows immediately behind Valerio.
(B) Ovitz rows immediately behind Valerio.
(C) Ovitz rows immediately behind Zita.
(D) Valerio rows immediately behind Lee.
(E) Singh rows immediately behind Zita.

9. Which one of the following CANNOT be true?

(A) Ovitz rows closer to the front than Singh.
(B) Zita rows closer to the front than Miller.
(C) Lee rows closer to the front than Valerio.
(D) Singh rows closer to the front than Zita.
(E) Valerio rows closer to the front than Lee.

10. Exactly how many different seats could be the seat occupied by Zita?

(A) two
(B) three
(C) four
(D) five
(E) six

11. If Valerio rows closer to the front than Zita, then which one of the following must be true?

(A) Miller rows immediately in front of Singh.
(B) Lee rows immediately in front of Valerio.
(C) Zita rows immediately in front of Ovitz.
(D) Singh rows immediately in front of Lee.
(E) Singh rows immediately in front of Valerio.

12. Suppose the restriction that Miller rows closer to the front than Singh is replaced by the restriction that Singh rows closer to the front than Miller. If the other two restrictions remain in effect, then each of the following could be an accurate matching of athletes to seats EXCEPT:

(A) Singh: seat 1; Zita: seat 2; Miller: seat 6
(B) Singh: seat 1; Valerio: seat 3; Ovitz: seat 5
(C) Singh: seat 3; Lee: seat 4; Valerio: seat 5
(D) Valerio: seat 3; Miller: seat 4; Lee: seat 5
(E) Valerio: seat 4; Miller: seat 5; Ovitz: seat 6

GO ON TO THE NEXT PAGE.

Questions 13–17

Exactly six of an artist's paintings, entitled *Quarterion*, *Redemption*, *Sipapu*, *Tesseract*, *Vale*, and *Zelkova*, are sold at auction. Three of the paintings are sold to a museum, and three are sold to a private collector. Two of the paintings are from the artist's first (earliest) period, two are from her second period, and two are from her third (most recent) period. The private collector and the museum each buy one painting from each period. The following conditions hold:

    Sipapu, which is sold to the private collector, is from an earlier period than *Zelkova*, which is sold to the museum.
    Quarterion is not from an earlier period than *Tesseract*.
    Vale is from the artist's second period.

13. Which one of the following could be an accurate list of the paintings bought by the museum and the private collector, listed in order of the paintings' periods, from first to third?

    (A)   museum: *Quarterion, Vale, Zelkova*
                 private collector: *Redemption, Sipapu, Tesseract*
    (B)   museum: *Redemption, Zelkova, Quarterion*
                 private collector: *Sipapu, Vale, Tesseract*
    (C)   museum: *Sipapu, Zelkova, Quarterion*
                 private collector: *Tesseract, Vale, Redemption*
    (D)   museum: *Tesseract, Quarterion, Zelkova*
                 private collector: *Sipapu, Redemption, Vale*
    (E)   museum: *Zelkova, Tesseract, Redemption*
                 private collector: *Sipapu, Vale, Quarterion*

14. If *Sipapu* is from the artist's second period, which one of the following could be two of the three paintings bought by the private collector?

    (A)   *Quarterion* and *Zelkova*
    (B)   *Redemption* and *Tesseract*
    (C)   *Redemption* and *Vale*
    (D)   *Redemption* and *Zelkova*
    (E)   *Tesseract* and *Zelkova*

15. Which one of the following is a complete and accurate list of the paintings, any one of which could be the painting from the artist's first period that is sold to the private collector?

    (A)   *Quarterion, Redemption*
    (B)   *Redemption, Sipapu*
    (C)   *Quarterion, Sipapu, Tesseract*
    (D)   *Quarterion, Redemption, Sipapu, Tesseract*
    (E)   *Redemption, Sipapu, Tesseract, Zelkova*

16. If *Sipapu* is from the artist's second period, then which one of the following paintings could be from the period immediately preceding *Quarterion*'s period and be sold to the same buyer as *Quarterion*?

    (A)   *Redemption*
    (B)   *Sipapu*
    (C)   *Tesseract*
    (D)   *Vale*
    (E)   *Zelkova*

17. If *Zelkova* is sold to the same buyer as *Tesseract* and is from the period immediately preceding *Tesseract*'s period, then which one of the following must be true?

    (A)   *Quarterion* is sold to the museum.
    (B)   *Quarterion* is from the artist's third period.
    (C)   *Redemption* is sold to the private collector.
    (D)   *Redemption* is from the artist's third period.
    (E)   *Redemption* is sold to the same buyer as *Vale*.

GO ON TO THE NEXT PAGE.

Questions 18–22

Each of exactly six lunch trucks sells a different one of six kinds of food: falafel, hot dogs, ice cream, pitas, salad, or tacos. Each truck serves one or more of exactly three office buildings: X, Y, or Z. The following conditions apply:

The falafel truck, the hot dog truck, and exactly one other truck each serve Y.

The falafel truck serves exactly two of the office buildings.

The ice cream truck serves more of the office buildings than the salad truck.

The taco truck does not serve Y.

The falafel truck does not serve any office building that the pita truck serves.

The taco truck serves two office buildings that are also served by the ice cream truck.

18. Which one of the following could be a complete and accurate list of each of the office buildings that the falafel truck serves?

(A)   X
(B)   X, Z
(C)   X, Y, Z
(D)   Y, Z
(E)   Z

19. For which one of the following pairs of trucks must it be the case that at least one of the office buildings is served by both of the trucks?

(A)   the hot dog truck and the pita truck
(B)   the hot dog truck and the taco truck
(C)   the ice cream truck and the pita truck
(D)   the ice cream truck and the salad truck
(E)   the salad truck and the taco truck

20. If the ice cream truck serves fewer of the office buildings than the hot dog truck, then which one of the following is a pair of lunch trucks that must serve exactly the same buildings as each other?

(A)   the falafel truck and the hot dog truck
(B)   the falafel truck and the salad truck
(C)   the ice cream truck and the pita truck
(D)   the ice cream truck and the salad truck
(E)   the ice cream truck and the taco truck

21. Which one of the following could be a complete and accurate list of the lunch trucks, each of which serves all three of the office buildings?

(A)   the hot dog truck, the ice cream truck
(B)   the hot dog truck, the salad truck
(C)   the ice cream truck, the taco truck
(D)   the hot dog truck, the ice cream truck, the pita truck
(E)   the ice cream truck, the pita truck, the salad truck

22. Which one of the following lunch trucks CANNOT serve both X and Z?

(A)   the hot dog truck
(B)   the ice cream truck
(C)   the pita truck
(D)   the salad truck
(E)   the taco truck

S T O P

IF YOU FINISH BEFORE TIME IS CALLED, YOU MAY CHECK YOUR WORK ON THIS SECTION ONLY.
DO NOT WORK ON ANY OTHER SECTION IN THE TEST.

Acknowledgment is made to the following sources from which material has been adapted for use in this test booklet:

Wilfred L. Guerin et al., *A Handbook of Critical Approaches to Literature*. ©1966, 1979 by Wilfred L. Guerin, Earle Labor, Lee Morgan, and John R. Willingham.

Miwa Nishimura, "Japanese/English Code-Switching: Syntax and Pragmatics." ©1995 by Miwa Nishimura.

Michael A. Olivas, "The Political Economy of Immigration, Intellectual Property, and Racial Harassment: Case Studies of the Implementation of Legal Change on Campus." ©1992 by the Ohio State University Press.

Wait for the supervisor's instructions before you open the page to the topic.
Please print and sign your name and write the date in the designated spaces below.
Time: 35 Minutes

General Directions

You will have 35 minutes in which to plan and write an essay on the topic inside. Read the topic and the accompanying directions carefully. You will probably find it best to spend a few minutes considering the topic and organizing your thoughts before you begin writing. In your essay, be sure to develop your ideas fully, leaving time, if possible, to review what you have written. **Do not write on a topic other than the one specified. Writing on a topic of your own choice is not acceptable.**

No special knowledge is required or expected for this writing exercise. Law schools are interested in the reasoning, clarity, organization, language usage, and writing mechanics displayed in your essay. How well you write is more important than how much you write.

Confine your essay to the blocked, lined area on the front and back of the separate writing sample response sheet. Only that area will be reproduced for law schools. Be sure that your writing is legible.

Both this topic sheet and your response sheet must be turned over to the testing staff before you leave the room.

LSAC®

Topic Code

Date
/   /

Print Your Full Name Here		
Last	First	M.I.

Sign Your Name Here

Scratch Paper
Do not write your essay in this space.

LSAT® Writing Sample Topic

Alma owns a small art gallery that is situated in the middle of a busy commercial district. She is considering two different approaches to adding to the inventory of pieces she offers for sale. Write an essay in which you argue for one plan over the other, keeping in mind the following goals:

- Alma would like to specialize in locally produced artwork.
- The new items should attract new customers.

In the first plan, Alma would introduce a line of metalwork sculptures, made available through a regional consortium of artists, to fill a gap in her inventory for small, affordable gift items. Initially, the items would bring in new business from existing foot traffic and from those browsing or shopping during the lunch hour. Should these pieces do well, she would then bring in additional small-scale artwork in the hopes of establishing herself more firmly in the market for smaller pieces. Although Alma would be able to cater to a wider customer base, she would have competition from several stores in the area that also offer small gift items, although none specializes in the original artwork of local artists.

In the second plan, Alma would take advantage of an opportunity to become the sole representative for the artwork in the estate of a deceased painter whose works are now being valued at ever increasing amounts. The painter lived most of his life in the area, but his later works, making up most of the paintings in the estate, were actually painted elsewhere. By becoming the sole representative for the painter's work, she would acquire a limited collection of paintings for which there is a well-established niche market. The art gallery presently has only a small number of very expensive pieces, but attracting this small, specialized clientele would give Alma an established audience for other high-end works she might acquire in the future.

WP-L028-A

Scratch Paper
Do not write your essay in this space.

LAST NAME (Print)

FIRST NAME (Print)

SSN/ SIN

L

MI

TEST CENTER NO.

SIGNATURE

M M D D Y Y

TEST DATE

LSAC ACCOUNT NO.

TOPIC CODE

Writing Sample Response Sheet

DO NOT WRITE IN THIS SPACE

Begin your essay in the lined area below.
Continue on the back if you need more space.

Directions:

1. Use the Answer Key on the next page to check your answers.

2. Use the Scoring Worksheet below to compute your raw score.

3. Use the Score Conversion Chart to convert your raw score into the 120-180 scale.

Scoring Worksheet

1. Enter the number of questions you answered correctly in each section.

	Number Correct
SECTION I	_____
SECTION II	_____
SECTION III.	_____
SECTION IV.	_____

2. Enter the sum here: _____
   This is your Raw Score.

Conversion Chart
For Converting Raw Score to the 120-180 LSAT Scaled Score
LSAT Form 5LSN67

Reported Score	Raw Score Lowest	Raw Score Highest
180	99	101
179	98	98
178	97	97
177	96	96
176	95	95
175	94	94
174	93	93
173	92	92
172	91	91
171	90	90
170	89	89
169	88	88
168	86	87
167	85	85
166	84	84
165	82	83
164	81	81
163	79	80
162	78	78
161	76	77
160	75	75
159	73	74
158	71	72
157	70	70
156	68	69
155	67	67
154	65	66
153	63	64
152	62	62
151	60	61
150	58	59
149	57	57
148	55	56
147	53	54
146	51	52
145	50	50
144	48	49
143	46	47
142	45	45
141	43	44
140	42	42
139	40	41
138	38	39
137	37	37
136	35	36
135	34	34
134	33	33
133	31	32
132	30	30
131	28	29
130	27	27
129	26	26
128	25	25
127	23	24
126	22	22
125	21	21
124	20	20
123	18	19
122	17	17
121	16	16
120	0	15

SECTION I

1.	D	8.	D	15.	E	22.	D
2.	E	9.	C	16.	B	23.	A
3.	C	10.	D	17.	A	24.	B
4.	B	11.	E	18.	D	25.	D
5.	E	12.	B	19.	B	26.	E
6.	E	13.	A	20.	B	27.	A
7.	A	14.	E	21.	A	28.	E

SECTION II

1.	C	8.	C	15.	D	22.	A
2.	A	9.	D	16.	E	23.	D
3.	E	10.	A	17.	E	24.	C
4.	B	11.	E	18.	D	25.	C
5.	D	12.	B	19.	D		
6.	E	13.	D	20.	D		
7.	C	14.	C	21.	E		

SECTION III

1.	A	8.	C	15.	D	22.	D
2.	E	9.	A	16.	B	23.	B
3.	B	10.	B	17.	E	24.	B
4.	C	11.	D	18.	B	25.	A
5.	E	12.	C	19.	B	26.	E
6.	E	13.	A	20.	E		
7.	D	14.	C	21.	B		

SECTION IV

1.	D	8.	E	15.	D	22.	C
2.	E	9.	A	16.	B		
3.	A	10.	D	17.	B		
4.	E	11.	A	18.	D		
5.	B	12.	C	19.	C		
6.	C	13.	B	20.	E		
7.	E	14.	B	21.	A		

LSAT® **PREP TOOLS**

New! The Official LSAT Handbook

Get to know the LSAT

The LSAT is a test of analytical reasoning, logical reasoning, and reading comprehension, including comparative reading. What's the best way to learn how to approach these types of questions *before* you encounter them on the day of the test? There's no better way than The Official LSAT Handbook, published by the Law School Admission Council, the organization that produces the LSAT. This inexpensive guide will introduce you to the skills that the LSAT is designed to assess so that you can make the most of the rest of your test preparation and do your best on the test. (Note: This handbook contains information that is also included in The Official LSAT SuperPrep. The information in The Official LSAT Handbook has been expanded and updated since it was first published in The Official LSAT SuperPrep.)

$12 ($9.95 online)

LSAC.org